The Modern Nations in
Historical Perspective

Robin W. Winks, General Editor

The volumes in this series deal with individual nations or groups of closely related nations throughout the world, summarizing the chief historical trends and influences that have contributed to each nation's present-day character, problems, and behavior. Recent data are incorporated with established historical background to achieve a fresh synthesis and original interpretation.

BARRY GOUGH, *Associate Professor of History at Wilfrid Laurier University, Waterloo, Ontario, has had visiting appointments at Duke University and the University of Victoria. A Canadian, he has taught at universities in Canada and the United States, has a longstanding interest in Canadian-American relations, and is actively involved in professional societies dedicated to the ideal of Canadian-American understanding. Dr. Gough is the author of* The Royal Navy and the Northwest Coast of North America *and* To the Arctic and Pacific with Beechey.

BOOKS IN THE COMMONWEALTH SUBSERIES

Australia *by Russel Ward*
Canada *by Barry M. Gough*
New Zealand *by William J. Cameron*

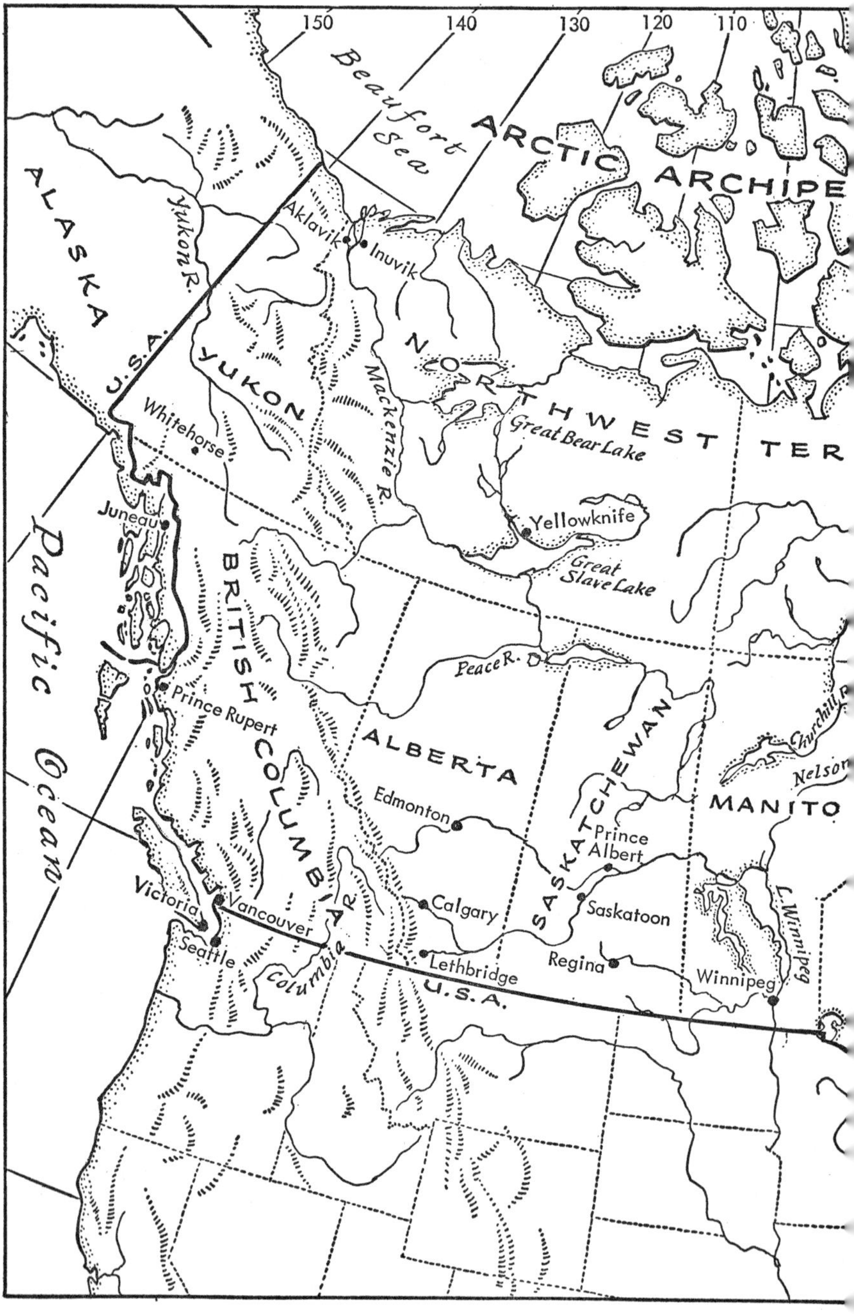

150
140
130
120
110
Beaufort Sea
ARCTIC ARCHIPE
ALASKA
Yukon R.
Aklavik
Inuvik
U.S.A.
YUKON
Mackenzie R.
NORTHWEST TER
Whitehorse
Great Bear Lake
Juneau
Yellowknife
Great Slave Lake
Pacific Ocean
BRITISH COLUMBIA
Peace R.
Prince Rupert
ALBERTA
SASKATCHEWAN
Churchill R.
Nelson
MANITO
Edmonton
Prince Albert
Victoria
Vancouver
Calgary
Saskatoon
L. Winnipeg
Seattle
Columbia R.
Lethbridge
Regina
Winnipeg
U.S.A.

CANADA
0
200
400
600
800 miles
Baffin Bay
Davis Strait
GREENLAND
Atlantic Ocean
Hudson Strait
UNGAVA PEN.
Hudson Bay
LABRADOR
NEWFOUNDLAND
QUEBEC
James Bay
ONTARIO
N.F.
St. John's
PR. EDWARD I.
Charlottetown
MIQUELON
ST. PIERRE
NEW BRUNSWICK
NOVA SCOTIA
Halifax
Fredericton
St. John
Quebec
Montreal
Ottawa
St. Lawrence R.
U.S.A.
Boston
New York
Sault Ste. Marie
Sudbury
L. Superior
L. Huron
L. Michigan
L. Ontario
L. Erie
Toronto
Hamilton
Detroit
Windsor
Bay
80
60
40
50

EASTERN NORTH AMERICA
—1763—
British possessions
French "
Spanish "
0 200 400 600 miles
Hudson Bay
RUPERT'S LAND
(HUDSON'S BAY COMPANY)
(LABRADOR) NEWFOUNDLAND
FRENCH SHORE
ST. PIERRE ET MIQUELON (FRANCE)
CAPE BRETON I.
ST. JOHN
NOVA SCOTIA
Halifax
QUEBEC
Quebec
Montreal
St. Lawrence R.
INDIAN TERRITORY
L. Superior
L. Michigan
L. Huron
L. Ontario
L. Erie
Detroit
Mississippi R.
Missouri R.
LOUISIANA
Ohio R.
Tennessee R.
PROCLAMATION LINE
THE THIRTEEN COLONIES
Boston
New York
Atlantic Ocean
Charleston
Savannah
WEST FLORIDA
New Orleans
EAST FLORIDA
Gulf of Mexico
BAHAMA IS.
CUBA
JAMAICA
ST. DOMINGUE
PORTO RICO
MEXICO
80
60
50
40
20

The Modern Nations in Historical Perspective

CANADA

Barry Gough

PRENTICE-HALL, INC. A SPECTRUM BOOK *Englewood Cliffs, New Jersey*

Library of Congress Cataloging in Publication Data

Gough, Barry
Canada.

(The Modern nations in historical perspective)
(A Spectrum book)
Bibliography: p.
Includes index.
1. Canada—History.
F1026.G68 917.1'03 74-30324
ISBN 0-13-112789-6
ISBN 0-13-112771-3 pbk.

Grateful acknowledgment is made for permission to reproduce copyrighted materials in this book:

To the Minnesota Historical Society, for excerpts from W. L. Morton, "The North West Company: Pedlars Extraordinary," *Minnesota History*, XL (Winter 1966); to Malcolm Ross, for excerpts from his preface to *Our Sense of Identity: A Book of Canadian Essays* (Toronto: Ryerson Press, 1954); to CBC Publications, for excerpts from Frank H. Underhill, *The Image of Confederation.* The Massey Letters, 1963 (1964); to The Canadian Publishers, McClelland & Stewart Ltd., Toronto, for excerpts from Hilda Neatby, *Quebec, The Revolutionary Age, 1760–1791* (1966); to the University of Toronto Press, for excerpts from Andrew Hill Clark, *Three Centuries and the Island: A Historical Geography of Settlement and Agriculture in Prince Edward Island, Canada* (1959) and Peter B. Waite, *The Life and Times of Confederation, 1864–1867: Politics, Newspapers, and the Union of British North America* (1962); to Macmillan of Canada, for excerpts from Pierre Elliott Trudeau, *Federalism and the French Canadians* (1968) and H. Blair Neatby, *The Politics of Chaos: Canada in the Thirties* (1972); to Charles Scribner's Sons, New York, for excerpts from Hugh MacLennan, *The Watch that Ends the Night* (1959); to Holt, Rinehart and Winston of Canada, Limited, Toronto, for excerpts from Marcel Trudel, *Introduction to New France* (1968); to the University of Washington Press, Seattle and London, for excerpts from S. F. Wise and R. Craig Brown, *Canada Views the United States: Nineteenth-Century Political Attitudes* (1967); to Viking Press, Inc., New York, for excerpts from Wallace Stegner, *Wolf Willow* (1962); to Farrar, Straus and Giroux, Inc., New York, for excerpts from Edmund Wilson, *O Canada: An American's Notes on Canadian Culture* (1964).

10 9 8 7 6 5 4 3 2 1

Prentice-Hall International, Inc. (*London*)
Prentice-Hall of Australia Pty. Ltd. (*Sydney*)
Prentice-Hall of Canada Ltd. (*Toronto*)
Prentice-Hall of India Private Limited (*New Delhi*)
Prentice-Hall of Japan, Inc. (*Tokyo*)

Contents

Foreword & Preface

Professor Barry M. Gough's history of Canada joins eight other volumes in comprising the Commonwealth sub-set in the Modern Nations in Historical Perspective series (three more Commonwealth volumes are projected). In many ways, the present volume is one of the most important in the series, for it deals with the nation that rightly can consider itself to be the Mother Dominion. Of the many clear precedents by which a colony became an independent nation, during the period when the Westminster model of Parliament was being transferred overseas, most of these precedents arose in Canada, through Canadian action, or as a result of a Canadian event. Put differently, if one is to understand the evolution of parliamentary government in Nigeria, or Kenya, or Australia, one must begin with the Canadian models and, thus, with Canadian history. Hence, the history of Canada stands central to the history of the British empire and the later Commonwealth.

Canada is important in a second way. Sharing the North American continent with a large and expansive neighbor, Canadians have had to learn how to mediate between the cultures of the United States and those of Britain and France. This has led to the development of a unique political and social history for Canada. Yet, sharing the same general environment, Canada also has developed along some lines that show similarities to developments in the United States. Thus, Canada is an ideal nation to which one may apply the techniques of comparative history, and the Canadian story—intertwined as it is with the history of the United States—aptly illustrates the importance of discarding the old Whiggish bias by which we organize history into national units, as though the rise of the nation state were the only purpose to historical causation. In short, the history of Canada helps test several elements in the conventional wisdom of the past and helps us to reformulate our views on the historical perspective of modern nationalism and nationhood.

ROBIN W. WINKS
General Editor

This book seeks to portray in brief compass the main themes of Canadian history. It aims to describe the historical trends and influences that have led to Canada's current character, problems, and behavior. These include the role of environment and frontier; the complex relationship between English and French Canadians and their ongoing relationships with other ethnic groups; the hard realities and sustained myths of Canada's relationship with the United States since 1776; the unique features of regionalism in Canadian life and the attendant difficulties in federal-provincial relations and national economic development; and finally, the growth of a Canadian political and cultural identity.

By focusing on these themes it is hoped that the critical issues of Canadian history—issues which pervade the everyday lives of Canadians—may be brought to life and emphasized. In keeping with this objective, I have had to sacrifice attention to a number of developments of secondary importance. However, in the section "Suggested Readings," which follows the text, readers will find mention of works that will supplement and amplify the material contained in this volume. During the writing of this book I have profited from the advice of colleagues, readers, and students but I alone am responsible for the contents.

BARRY GOUGH

For Louise, Melinda, and Jason

1

Historical Perspectives and Issues

Among the histories of the nation-states of the modern world, that of Canada is likely to be either not well known or misunderstood. In the United States, for instance, the nuances of the Canadian experience have often been missed or neglected altogether. The great American man of letters, Edmund Wilson, wrote that in his youth, during the early 1900s, Americans never paid much attention to Canada. For him, Canada was "an inconceivably limitless extension of the wilderness of upstate New York," a kind of "vast hunting preserve convenient to the United States." [1] Wilson himself was to learn a good deal about Canada, to come to understand the particularities of Canadian life, and to note the differences (not easily found) that separate Canadians from Americans. Recently, Americans have wanted to know more about Canada, and in time their stereotyped view of the land of Rose Marie, Sergeant Preston, and endless igloos will be modified.

Canadians themselves are not fully conversant with the intrica-

1. O *Canada: An American's Notes on Canadian Culture* (New York: Farrar, Straus and Giroux, 1964), pp. 36, 37.

cies and problems of their own history. If recent studies emanating from royal commissions and educational institutes are any indication, the study of Canada past and present is being insufficiently dealt with in Canadian schools and universities. But the search for the visible past is not without reward: Canadian heroes appear where previously the public had expected none; the drama of national development, warts and all, unfolds where none was anticipated; and the peculiarities of a complex society are revealed where before a disparate amalgam had existed in many minds. To Canadians and non-Canadians then, the study of this unique nation's history is rewarding for those patient enough to undertake it.

Such a study soon brings into view two interrelated myths: that Canada is both underdeveloped and underpopulated. In fact, this country is among the most developed of Western societies and has a sufficient population for her extensive resource-extractive industry. Canada is one of the principal trading partners in the modern world, and her economy continues to develop in relationship to world and continental markets. This type of economy needs capital, technology, and expertise, of course, but requires little manpower in comparison with an agricultural or even a heavy industry economy. Although Canada lacks neither agriculture nor heavy industry in relation to her population base, the chief means of her existence among nation-states is trade in natural products of the earth, sea and forest such as pulp and paper, oil and gas, uranium and nickel, fish and grains.

Canadian society is perforce diverse. Huge urban complexes such as Montreal, Toronto, and Vancouver, each with populations in the millions, have developed at great places of trade—all on or adjacent to the great sea-lanes of the world. Smaller cities and towns have come into existence as places of commerce. Even smaller settlements of several hundred persons exist as places of production, agriculture, or extraction. On a per capita basis probably no people in the world control more of the globe's land surface than do Canadians. According to the 1971 census the government of some 22 million persons has sovereignty over 3,852,000 square miles of northern North America. However, Canadians are among the world's most urbanized peoples; they live primarily in a small ribbon of land, perhaps 100 miles wide, hugging the northern boundary of the United States—this for good reason. The interplays of environment and regionalism, of frontier and metropolis, and of race and national identity have combined forces to shape a small, urban, modern, highly technical society.

Environment and Regionalism

From earliest times the Canadian experience has been a Northern, Arctic one. Canada is a Northern country with a Northern economy. It has a Northern way of life. It has a Northern destiny. The Northern imperative has been a psychological drive to Canadians. Siegfried, the French political analyst, put it this way:

> No Canadian will ever disown the North, for to him it is a boundless territory of unknown possibilities. Doubtless it is some obscure instinct that makes him resent as a criticism any remark by a foreigner about the severity of these lands which in truth do demand the maximum of man's energy. They have never forgiven Voltaire for referring to their country as "a few acres of snow," and many are still angry over the vigorous description of the rude life of the pioneers around Lake St. John given in *Maria Chapdelaine*. Yet the North is always there like a presence; it is the background of the picture without which Canada would not be Canada.[2]

Such Canadian sensitivities toward the North have been stated in various works, and numerous book titles reflect the Northern focus of Canadian writers. And in the visual arts, music, and architecture, "Northern-ness" is often the all-pervading and persuasive theme.

This is not without accident, of course, for Canada's climate, landscape, and vegetation are Northern. Generally speaking, only in Canada's most southern latitudes and consequently only near the American border does one find a subsoil never frozen and consequently suitable for agriculture. The Annapolis, St. Lawrence, Saskatchewan, and Fraser are the main valleys in which agricultural pro-

2. André Siegfried, *Canada: An International Power,* 2nd ed., transl. Doris Hemming (London: Jonathan Cape, 1949), p. 26. See also essays by W. L. Morton, R. H. Hubbard, and Desmond Pacey (on the influence of the Canadian north on Canadian historiography, architecture, and literature) in *Transactions of the Royal Society of Canada,* series iv, vol. viii (1970).

duction is intensive and supports its population. Only the short-grass plains of Alberta, Saskatchewan, and Manitoba produce a grain surplus. Elsewhere, especially in British Columbia and the middle and extreme North, mining and other resource-centered industries such as hydropower, pulp and paper production, and petroleum extraction from wells and tar sands provide the principal occupations.

Considered from another perspective, Canada does not have an extensive central alluvial basin such as the Mississippi capable of supporting a large settlement population. Rather, its principal geographical feature is the Precambrian or Canadian Shield. This vast structure of granite and gneiss around which the geological structure of North America is anchored was at the time of European-Amerind contact the home of numerous tribes who in due course would share their woodland skills with the Europeans. Along the Shield's forested southern margin Indians and fur traders in their superb canoes used a natural though intricate east–west route. This so called Voyageurs' Highway linked together Lakes Superior, Winnipeg, and Athabaska. These lakes were the hubs of three low-elevation drainage saucers leading respectively to the Gulf of St. Lawrence, Hudson Strait, and the mouth of the Mackenzie River. This trunk system and its numerous branch routes provided the first transcontinental Canadian business route joining the St. Lawrence with the Fraser and Columbia rivers of the Pacific slope. This throughway was developed some thirty years before American settlers crossed the Mississippi. The occupation of wooded and well-watered lands highly suitable for the fur trade resulted in a different frontier experience than that of the Americans in the Mississippi valley. Here then is one of the features of Canadian history: environment produced a unique frontier experience. The fur trade, the first staple yield of the Canadian hinterland, was followed by other staple trades that would expand and modify this east–west network.

Environmental circumstances have also given rise to extensive regionalism. Obviously, man's relationship to his environment and to the economic structure of the country determines his perception of what his nation means to him. The regions of Canada—the Pacific Cordillera, the Prairies, the St. Lawrence Valley, the Maritimes, and the North, including the Precambrian shield—have all fostered local identities. To a British Columbian, the Pacific Ocean, the Rocky

Mountain Cordillera, and his insularity from Central Canada have fostered a local perspective. To a resident of Alberta, Saskatchewan, or Manitoba, the interplay of spacious prairie and continental climate has produced a strong identity. To the occupants of the St. Lawrence Valley, English-speaking and French-speaking alike, the common denominator, the River St. Lawrence, has given a central position in the transcontinental Canadian experience, though language and race provide critical divisions. To Maritimers, their position on or near the North Atlantic and their relative insularity from Central Canada and one another has brought a particular perception of what constitutes a Canadian. And to inhabitants of the Canadian North, climate and economic opportunity, government input, and corporate development provide an emerging regionalism.

In each of these areas, the occupants are developing what can be called "limited identities." Thus what Canada means to a person living in Ontario is quite different from what it means to a Newfoundlander, Quebecois, or Manitoban. Within these regions, subidentities exist and are defined—in the case of the St. Lawrence Valley, for example, by ethnic factors. Canada is a land of particularism and, one might add, in some cases, local prejudice. Regional and centrifugal pulls have been reflected in the rise of provincial powers since the confederation of British North America in 1867. In the Maritimes an ongoing protest movement exists against Ontario and its industry. The Prairie provinces have a similar perspective, with complaints emanating particularly from Western farmers and oilmen against "the vested interests of the East." Quebec has its own economic complaints, as does British Columbia. And from time to time Ontario has been in the vanguard of the movement for provincial rights against centralism in the national capital at Ottawa.

Nonetheless, through the hard workings of provincial-federal relations, the federal structure evolves and shifts. Limited identities have produced a transcontinental creation unique in its compromises and pluralism. If Canadian federalism were finite, the country would long ago have disintegrated. But it is organic, changing with the political needs of the day and adapting to the central and peripheral tendencies of the times. When A. R. M. Lower observed that the writing of Canadian history was "an act of faith, the substance of things hoped for," he put his finger on one of the essential features of the

Canadian experience: the lack of fusion in Canada.[3] Disparate and divided by geography and race, Canadians have in their historical backgrounds deeply based regionalisms. These regionalisms are founded in their individual experiences that date in some cases from colonial times.

Frontier and Metropolis

We have already seen how geography and environment have contributed to the Northern and regional character of Canada. We must now direct our attention to a related matter: how Canada has historically been part of a frontier—in fact, part of three frontiers. Like Russia, Australia, and the United States, where the process of the frontier played a large role in shaping national development and identity, Canada has had its own unique frontiers. The first frontier came from Asia during prehistoric times. In terminal Pleistocene–early Holocene times, persons of basically Mesolithic culture crossed Beringia from Siberia and penetrated into the Pacific Cordillera. Later, ancestral Aleut and Eskimo came to northern North America. Subsequently, populous Amerind societies inhabited the western coast, central plains, and eastern woodlands. At the time of European contact, the Amerind population of what now constitutes Canada approximated 221,000.

The second frontier affecting Canada involved the European penetration of the continent. This began with the Norse expansion across the North Atlantic from Scandinavia to Iceland, Greenland, Baffin Island, and Newfoundland. This approach took on a different form in the seventeenth through nineteenth centuries, when the French and British penetrated the continent. This advance of a technologically superior culture from northwestern Europe spelled the tragic collapse of Indian and Eskimo political structures and life styles. And smallpox and other diseases introduced by Europeans greatly reduced aboriginal populations. This second frontier consisted of several phases: first, the maritime process, similar to the Norse expansion, which culminated in extensive northward exploration and the establishment of pocket settlements, trading posts, and

3. In the preface to *Colony to Nation: A History of Canada*, 4th ed., rev. (Toronto: Longman Canada, Ltd., 1971), p. xi.

missions in the Bay of Fundy, banks of the St. Lawrence, and Hudson Bay; second, the subsequent settling of arable lands in Acadia and the St. Lawrence Valley in the period from 1783 to 1850; third, the advance on the Canadian far West and prairie West in the late eighteenth and nineteenth centuries, an approach made overland from Montreal and Hudson Bay and by sea via long sea-lanes to the northwest coast of North America; fourth, the occupation of the "last, best West" of Canadian prairie in the nineteenth century, which was perhaps as closely tied to the American western development as any; and finally, the advance, still underway, on the far North.

Canada's third frontier has not emanated from overseas; rather, it has been a landed frontier from the United States. Loyalist immigration into British North America after the American Revolution made a profound impact on the political and social development of Canada, particularly on Upper Canada and New Brunswick. This frontier also contributed to a war, in the years 1812 to 1814, which in turn influenced British American perceptions of American society and democracy. During most of the nineteenth century "Manifest Destiny" posed a threat to Canada and the British Empire provided Canada with security. The American military threat diminished in the early twentieth century. After 1945, however, American economic and cultural penetration of Canada accelerated markedly. As a place for investment and trade, Canada became an integral part of the informal American empire.

These three dominating frontiers have meant that, in turn, Paris, London, and New York have been the country's corporate centers, to which Canadians have gone for credit and capital. There, also, decisions have been made that have influenced the course of national development over the past four centuries. In Canada, various metropolitan centers—Montreal, Toronto, and Vancouver—have emerged to do the nation's business at home. In addition, other regional centers have emerged such as Halifax, Winnipeg, and Prince George, each serving vast hinterlands. These frontiers have all involved the relationship of metropolis, metropolitan markets, and hinterland. Staple trades—in fur, timber, pulp and paper, grains, hydropower, oils, and so on—have also had a part in the development of the Canadian frontier. Transportation by rivers, lakes, and oceans have made the Canadian frontier experience very much a maritime one. The development of portages, canals, seaways, and new modes of bulk and container shipping have assisted in the exporting of staples and the importing of trade items.

Linked with the growth of seaborne trade has been the development of new modes of transportation overland. The Voyageurs' Highway was succeeded by wagon roads and railways which adhered very closely to the transcontinental water throughghway. Railways in particular have been important in Canada since the 1830s. Confederation was a creation of the railway age, and the future of the new dominion was predicated on the expansion of railways with the dual object of overcoming regionalism and outflanking the expansive Americans on the south and on the north in Alaska. New modes of transportation by road modified the economy substantially. In 1962 the Trans-Canada highway was completed, and in the period after 1945 truck transport expanded rapidly. Air cargo and passenger transport also grew, making the Northern frontier more accessible. And new modes of communication in which Canada was sometimes a pioneer allowed Canadians to do business across a country stretching some 3,500 miles from sea to sea and from the 49th parallel to the northernmost fringe of the Arctic Islands.

Though frontiers and environment have greatly influenced Canada and will continue to do so, it must be mentioned that Canada is not just "colonial." She is "imperial" because she has her own frontier abroad; she is part of the North American industrial heartland which, with Western Europe, dominates the wider world. It is one of the ironies of the Canadian experience then that although Canadians may feel they are being exploited by American and other foreign interests at home, they are in fact part, albeit a small part, of the large exploitation of world markets and sources of supply. Technology and geography have brought Canada into alignment with the United States in relation to the rest of the world. This arrangement allows Canadians to enjoy one of the best standards of living in the world. Nevertheless, living next to the colossus of the modern world has been a painful and unpleasant process for many Canadians, who feel that their sovereignty has been compromised by the sheer influence of the United States in the Western hemisphere and elsewhere, to say nothing of the impact of American popular culture at home.

However, as long as "bread and butter" matters remain paramount in Canadian minds, it seems unlikely that any departure from the third frontier will be taken. Growing economies, full employment, the free flow of capital—these are features of North American business; and it is because Canada and the United States share this ideology that Canada may long remain part of the American frontier.

Race and National Identity

Though powerful influences of the American frontier are exerted on Canada, an obstacle of equal difficulty in developing national self-interest is racial dualism. French and English languages exist side by side in Canada, in fact and in law. The result—the primary antithesis of Canadian history—has been two corresponding religious cultures, outlooks, and traditions. Each province has English- and French-speaking persons. However, in every province except Quebec, French are in a minority. In New Brunswick, the French minority accounts for nearly 40 percent of the population. This division of Canada into two racial fragments is at once the strength and the weakness of the country. It is the strength in that it makes Canada, generally speaking, the only non-unilingual nation in North America, a fact that allows the nation to be unique vis-à-vis the United States and Mexico. It is the weakness in that it can make unilingual Canadians foreigners in their own country. Racial animosities, fear, and prejudice run high in Canada. Minority rights issues have frequently become major political crises. Thus Canada is no happy union of the two societies under what the Fathers of Confederation in 1867 hoped would become "a new nationality." Instead it is a land in which racial clashes and deep divisions periodically appear, especially in time of war.

This dual character of Canadian society has allowed for a different type of political culture than in the United States. Minority rights have been enshrined in various legal and constitutional provisions. Most notable of these is Section 93 of the British North America Act (1867), which allows first that each provincial legislature may define its educational system and second that minorities within each province have certain safeguards and rights of appeal to the federal government. The result has been that protective measures have developed to allow minorities to have instruction in church-related schools. The overall tendency has not been to develop a "melting pot" along American lines (although of course we now know that the melting pot has numerous cracks) but rather to develop a "mosaic" in which cultures of various national backgrounds can exist without being completely absorbed by either French or English cultures. Pressure exerted by Ukranian, German, and other identities on the federal government have also deterred the advance of a melting pot in Canada. The possibility of a pluralistic society remains, with all its attendant problems for national unity. Pierre Elliott Trudeau, writing in *Cité Libre* in 1962, argued that Canada had the opportunity to be a model pluralistic society. In this French Canadians would have to mount a presence in Ottawa and English Canadians would have "to retire gracefully to their proper place, consenting to modify their own previous image of what Canada ought to be. If they care to protect and realize their own special ethnic qualities, they should do so within this framework of regional and local autonomy rather than a pan-Canadian one." And he continued:

> The die is cast in Canada: there are two main ethnic and linguistic groups; each is too strong and too deeply rooted in the past, too firmly bound to a mother-culture, to be able to engulf the other. But if the two will collaborate at the hub of a truly pluralistic state, Canada would become the envied seat of a form of federalism that belongs to tomorrow's world. Better than the American melting-pot, Canada could offer an example to all those new Asian and African states . . . who must discover how to govern their polyethnic populations with proper regard for justice and liberty. What better reason for cold-shouldering the lure of annexation to the United States? Canadian federalism is an experiment of major proportions; it could become a brilliant prototype for the moulding of tomorrow's civilization.[4]

But for reasons of race, Canada is more likely to remain an agglomeration of societies than a nation of common understanding and unity. Its political culture is divided by language, and both French and English political societies regard each other with some degree of suspicion.

4. "New Treason of the Intellectuals," in his *Federalism and the French Canadians* (Toronto: Macmillan of Canada, 1968), pp. 178–79.

In these circumstances, the Canadian identity can have no common ground. The result has been a mixed-bag culture. Rather than building from new Canadian foundations, Canadian authors have drawn heavily from the literary heritage of parent societies, especially France, the United States, and the United Kingdom. Indeed, because of the small domestic market, they have often written with foreign critics, publishers, and readers in mind. On the other hand, Canadian writers have habitually addressed themselves to two national issues. These are first, the harsh realities of the Canadian environment and second, the need to define Canada's identity. "Such has been the preoccupation with the question of Canada itself . . . that one is sometimes left with the odd sensation that Canada is nothing but a figment of the historical imagination." Such is the intimation of the *Literary History of Canada*.[5] But Malcolm Ross, a professor of English, put it differently. He noted that Canadian writing evidenced a North Americanism, but this was a Canadian, not an "American" variety. He writes:

> It is marked and structured by a phenomenon uniquely ours and the very contrary of the "melting pot" imperative of United States nationalism: The "two nations." The dual cultural and religious tradition. And the tension, the dynamic and fruitful tension, in play between the two. Baldwin–Lafontaine. Macdonald–Cartier. King–Lapointe. We are inescapably, and almost from the first, the bifocal people. The people of the second thought. To remain a people at all we have had to think before we speak, even to think before we think. Our "characteristic prudence" is not the Scot in us, or the Puritan, or the "North Irish." It is this bifocalism, this necessity for taking second thought, for keeping one foot on each bank of the Ottawa.[6]

In painting, poetry, drama, sculpture, and other arts the search for a national identity is going on. The painter Homer Watson, writ-

5. Carl L. Klinck et al., *Literary History of Canada: Canadian Literature in English* (Toronto: University of Toronto Press, 1965), quoted in a perceptive review of this book by Arlin Turner, "Literary History and National Identity: The Example of Canada," *The Southern Review*, new ser. VI, 2 (Spring 1970), 520–28.

6. Malcolm Ross, ed., *Our Sense of Identity: A Book of Canadian Essays* (Toronto: Ryerson Press, 1954), p. ix.

ing to his associate Arthur Lismer in 1930, thought this matter one of little consequence: "Myself being so much Canadian, why should I think of trying to be Canadian? . . . Things form naturally, not by forcing. . . . I was born amid the hardwood trees and noted the beech, oak and elm, as native as the jack pine. And the trees mentioned are not as those of England. There is a difference which I hope anyone with a discerning mind will see." [7] A national substitution of pleasure for pain might be realized if Canadians like Homer Watson learned that the Canadian past has resulted in a diverse, if somewhat precarious creation, a creation that can be lived with, a creation that ought not be rejected because it fails to fit the usual national stereotype. Canada as a unified, centralized political society and nation is elusive and will probably remain so for the future. A study of colonial and national developments, as outlined within this book, is intended to explain the particular problems and responses of modern Canada.

7. Quoted in Klinck et al., *Literary History of Canada,* p. x.

2

Colonial Origins to 1763

Canadian colonial origins date principally from the early seventeenth century. English and French navigators made reconnaissances in high latitudes and were followed by traders and settlers. By the mid-eighteenth century new societies had developed out of old as "fragments" of older cultures broke off from Europe, took root in America, and transformed themselves into new identities in the new land.[1]

What is unique about the early Canadian experience is that both French and English fragments took root. The French developed trade and settlement in Acadia and the St. Lawrence Valley; the English, in Hudson Bay and Newfoundland and eventually in Acadia and the St. Lawrence. The period of this development, lasting over two and a half centuries, resulted in the collapse of French empire and, correspondingly, the expansion of British colonial entities in northern North America. But it did not bring an end to the resilient French culture and language. Thus Canada's biracial essence and division originate in this period.

1. Louis Hartz et al., *The Founding of New Societies: Studies in the History of the United States, Latin America, South Africa, Canada and Australia* (New York: Harcourt, Brace and World, 1964), pp. 3–12. Compare Sidney F. Wise, "Conservatism and Political Development: The Canadian Case," *South Atlantic Quarterly*, LXIX, no. 2 (Spring 1970), pp. 226–43.

In 1523, twenty-six years after John Cabot had discovered Newfoundland for England and thirty-one after Columbus had claimed to have discovered the Indies for Spain, the French government sent Verrazano to find a northwest passage to the Orient. Why was France, the most populous of the Atlantic countries, the last to engage in westward discovery? The answer is that France's political and economic interests lay in the Mediterranean until news of Magellan's circumnavigation of 1519 to 1522 sparked the court's interest in the fabulous spice trade of the Orient. Verrazano's voyage was directly related to Magellan's. But the "blessed shores of Cathay" eluded him. Instead of finding a passage between Spanish Florida and Newfoundland that would have put France directly in contact with Asia, he found the American shoreline unyielding and its inhabitants in the New England area barbaric and intractable.

Yet Verrazano's navigations had uncovered a large land mass which merited closer investigation. The project for finding a direct route to Asia appealed to the king, Francis I. Jacques Cartier, a Breton mariner who had already sailed "to Brazil and the New Land," was entrusted to sail to "that realm of the *Terres Neufves* where it is said there must be great quantities of gold and other riches."

Cartier made three voyages. His first, in 1534, located the south shore and islands of the Gulf of St. Lawrence. There he found rocky, inhospitable land on the south shore which he believed was the one that God had reserved for Cain. At Gaspé on July 24 he erected a cross, contrary to the wishes of Chief Donnacona of the Iroquois. Shortly afterward he captured the chief's two sons and left for the North, having assured the father that they would return. Cartier missed discovering the St. Lawrence River because of bad weather. However, on his return to France he convinced the French court that his discovery of an inland sea, his alliance with the Indians, and the possibilities of a route to Asia and of commercial opportunity justified another attempt.

Cartier's second voyage brought him at last to the St. Lawrence, and his two Indian guides were the reason for his success. This river, they told him, was an ever-narrowing river to Canada and Hochelaga and was also a river of fresh water, one of which no man had ever been to the end. Donnacona's sons were soon reunited with their father and Cartier now moved upriver to Donnacona's cluster of huts called Stadacona and then to Hochelaga, a palisaded town of fifty houses lying below a mountain which Cartier named Mont Royal. From its height, Cartier could see the lay of the mountains on the north and south that bordered the St. Lawrence plain. And he could see the great cataract, the Lachine Rapids, situated on the river which, the Indians told him, could be navigated for three moons and more. This was Cartier's major discovery: a great river which in time would become the highway of French penetration into the hinterland.

On Cartier's third voyage, beginning in 1541, the first French colony was planted in North America. Spain meanwhile had protested to the French court and Rome that the western lands belonged to her. But, as Francis I replied, "to pass by and discover by eye is no title of possession." The pope, Paul III, did not object to France's claim, perhaps because he needed French support against the formidable power of Spain and because the expedition was sent under a strongly worded commission to extend the holy Christian faith in lands not already inhabited by any Christian prince. Thus did France penetrate lands which Spain thought reserved for itself.

The colonization was attempted under the leadership of Sieur de Roberval, a court favorite, with Cartier along as master pilot and guide. Several hundred soldiers, settlers both male and female, craftsmen and convicts—perhaps a thousand in all—along with cattle and two years' provisions, sailed from France to establish the first French colony in America. At Cap Rouge, near the Indian village of Stadacona, Cartier built a fort, and nearby, Roberval founded his colony called Charlesbourg Royal. The location was "a convenient place to fortifie ourselves in, fitted to command the mayne River, and of strong situation against all our enemies." The long Franco-Iroquois conflict began in the winter of 1541–1542, and the French held their position with their cannon. The heavy Laurentian winter took its toll on the settlers: scurvy, famine, and rebellion were the result and the colony withdrew after a few months.

Both Roberval and Cartier claimed to have found precious metals and stones. But the gold was actually iron pyrites while the diamonds were mica and this gave birth to the proverb "as false as Canadian diamonds." There were other disappointments. No easy passage to China existed beyond the Lachine Rapids. Indian promises of a wealthy Kingdom of the Saquenay also proved unfounded. Not surprisingly, French interest in Canada lay dormant for some fifty years as the kingdom was overcome by religious civil war. In any case, the Roberval-Cartier experiment had shown that great would have to be the resources, both human and material, if France were to colonize Canada.

Cod and Furs

Meanwhile, as French interest in North America waxed and waned, English interests grew and matured. Bristol fishermen may have discovered Newfoundland between 1480 and 1494 and, if so, the wealth of the Grand Banks (where shallow water, warm currents, and sunshine provided abundant plankton for cod) may have been known in England before John Cabot's famous voyage in 1497. In any case, Bristol merchants, alive to commercial possibilities, sent the Venetian navigator Cabot, under letters patent, to find and hold newly found lands and to discover a western sea route to Cathay in higher latitudes than had Columbus. Cabot's ship, the barque *Mathew,* made a landfall on June 24, 1497, and the place was most probably 52°22′ on the Labrador coast. During his coasting voyage, Cabot found the sea around Newfoundland "swimming with fish, which can be taken not only with the net but in baskets let down with a stone." Bristol fishermen now abandoned the less productive Iceland waters for the Grand Banks. In the early sixteenth century they were joined by other English fishermen and by the Portuguese, Bretons, and Spanish. These mariners were less interested in colonization than in the fishery: trade was their motivation, and cod, the first staple of the Canadian economy, became, in mercantile terms, a basis of profit and power for the nation that could control the Newfoundland fisheries.

In Elizabethan times, the English regarded the Newfoundland enterprise as the "nursery" of seamen, merchant shipping, and shipbuilding. It was one of the sinews of empire. The fishery became an element in the European balance of power in the conflict between England, France, and Spain. The island was thrice captured by the English, in 1697, 1708, and 1762. As Harold Innis, a shrewd analyst of Canadian economic history has written, "Cod from Newfoundland was the lever by which she [England] wrested her share of the riches of the New World from Spain." [2]

Initially, the English sought to control Newfoundland only as a fishing station, a place to dry the catch, and a "nursery of seamen." They did not seek to colonize it for this would have established a resident, competing fishery. "Britain's Oldest Colony" was therefore not a colony of settlement. In August 1583 Sir Humphrey Gilbert proclaimed English sovereignty over Newfoundland and twenty leagues around, which would have included parts of Nova Scotia, Cape Breton, and Labrador. He also issued regulations for the fishery and exercise of religion in conformity with the Church of England. He mined what he thought was silver but he planted no settlers. By the early seventeenth century, 200 English ships were fishing annually in Newfoundland waters.

This fishery drew the English increasingly in contact with the Beothuk Indians of Newfoundland, the original "redskins" of North America, who painted their faces with red dye. The English traded with them for furs. In Newfoundland, as along the coasts of the Gulf of St. Lawrence, white and native exchanged commodities which each had in abundance. In 1534 Cartier was trading in Chaleur Bay and the marketing techniques of the Indians indicated that he was not the first European to engage in the trade. Basques and Biscayans soon came there in growing numbers and gradually Tadoussac, near the mouth of the Saguenay, became the focal point of a fur empire stretching west and south to the Huron-Iroquois country on Georgian Bay. The empire of the St. Lawrence River was taking on new shape, and the fur trade, perhaps the main determinant in early Canadian history, was the reason for renewed French interest in the late sixteenth century.

By 1580 French merchants were outfitting expeditions for the St. Lawrence. Competition among them proved ruinous to the individual and state monopoly became the method for regulating the trade. In 1588 the Court granted it to Cartier's nephew, Noël, and his associate, La Jannaye, on condition that they settle the country and build forts. However, the king, Henry III, revoked his commission because of the protests of Saint Malo merchants who opposed colonization

2. Harold A. Innis, *The Cod Fisheries: The History of an International Economy* (New Haven: Yale University Press, 1940), p. 53.

and favored free trade. The conflict of fur trade and settlement had made its first appearance in North America.

But in 1597 a court favorite, the Marquis de La Roche, was appointed viceroy of French North American territories with the monopoly of the fur trade. He equipped an expedition which colonized the rocky Sable Island (off the east coast of Nova Scotia) with convicts. His monopoly, however, was undercut by a similar grant, in 1600, to Pierre Chauvin, an Honfleur merchant. He could engage in the St. Lawrence fishery but was obliged to send out fifty colonists each year. Disaster struck this enterprise and the trading monopoly fell to Sieur Pierre du Gua de Monts, in 1603.

De Monts, no stranger to Canada, overcame the difficulties of his unfortunate predecessors. He formed a small joint-stock company to fulfill the terms of the monopoly, which included taking out sixty colonists per year and converting Indians to the faith. By 1604 three of de Monts' ships were trading in the St. Lawrence while he himself, with his geographer and cartographer Samuel de Champlain, later termed the Father of New France, examined the Bay of Fundy and erected a fortification on the easily defensible St. Croix (or Dochet) Island. The party was sustained by the arrival of supply ships in early 1605. Champlain explored the New England coast and determined that French settlement there would conflict with that of the English. Thus de Monts decided to erect a habitation on the Annapolis Basin at what he called Port Royal. This became the first French settlement in North America. However, once again pressure from rival French merchants and nobles at court subverted the monopolists. De Monts then concentrated on the St. Lawrence and in 1608, on his instructions, Champlain built a fortification where the waters narrowed on the St. Lawrence, at Quebec.

The French focus was once again on the great river, the vestibule of commerce to the interior. In 1611, Champlain selected Montreal Island as a suitable site for a summer fur-trading post. There, in 1642, a settlement was established and put under the protection of the Virgin Mary, from whence it got its name: Ville Marie de Montréal. Under the co-leadership of Maisonneuve, working for the Association of Notre Dame for the Conversion of Savages of New France on the Island of Montreal, and of Jeanne Mance, who founded the hospital there, the settlement grew, if slowly. In 1660 the population was 350 in a village of forty dwellings. Defense against Indians remained a problem. As a Jesuit priest put it, "I would almost as soon be besieged by goblins as by the Iroquois. The latter are hardly more visible than the former." Nonetheless, situated to dominate the St. Lawrence and the hinterlands to the north, south, and west, Montreal, under good leadership and fur trade expansion, was to become a center of business, religion, and education. But downriver, at Quebec, lay the basis of the defense of New France.

It was from Quebec that Champlain went on to build the foundations of New France. From his headquarters at Quebec, he organized expeditions to ascend the St. Lawrence, expeditions intended to find an easy route to China and outflank the Spanish in North America. His explorations, beginning in 1609 into the *pays d'en haut*, or country upriver from Montreal, were several. His discoveries include the Ottawa River, Georgian Bay, Lake Ontario, and the Richelieu River–Lake Champlain region. His additions to European knowledge of North American geography were great, for he delineated the principal rivers and lakes of the St. Lawrence empire. By the 1740s his successors—La Salle and La Vérendrye—had uncovered most of the river secrets of the vast interior.

Race Relations

Champlain's expeditions perforce brought him into contact with various Indian tribes, the result being that the French found natural allies in the Huron, Algonkins, and Montagnais, who dominated the St. Lawrence system in and around Quebec. In 1609, for example, he set out with his allies to discover the Iroquois country by way of the Rivière des Iroquois (Richelieu). His group encountered the Iroquois, and a battle ensued in which Champlain's arquebus was first used. The Indian wars with European assistance had commenced and the use of firepower could now change the balance of power. This internecine war was already well advanced when Champlain founded Quebec; it existed because of the conflicting geographical interests of the St. Lawrence and Hudson watersheds. For the French, who were using the Ottawa River for their fur-trading route to the western tribes, the Huron became natural allies, while the Five Nations of the Iroquois posed as the military threat on the southern flank, capable of intercepting French supplies and furs at will as they passed down the St. Lawrence. Gradually, the French won the Iroquois as allies through gifts, treaties, and trade. But throughout much of the seventeenth century, and until a peace agreement between them was reached in 1701 the Iroquois held the French on sufferance.

In these circumstances it is easy to see why the French sought to have good relations with the Huron living in the triangular body of land between Lakes Huron and Erie. The Huron became the subject of sustained interest by the Society of Jesus. Members of this order, itself a product of the Counter-Reformation in Europe, had been in Canada periodically since 1613. With the establishment of their central mission at Ste. Marie on Georgian Bay in 1639, they commenced a plan to secure the St. Lawrence–Ottawa route. By 1649, 18 priests and 48 assistants were working in Huronia.

The difficulties the Jesuits faced in the wilderness among the "heathen" were enormous; and their *Relations*, published beginning in 1632, tell quite graphically of their existence among the Indians. The Indian often treated the missionary with barbarity: the martyrdom of Fathers Brébeuf and Lalement is as grueling a story as is recorded. And yet, the dismemberment of Ravillac, the assassin of Henry IV, in Paris, was no more saintly.

How did the French treat the Indians? Mason Wade, writing in 1969, could find little fault with Parkman's verdict of 1867 that while "Spanish civilization crushed the Indian; English civilization scorned and neglected him; French civilization embraced and cherished him." [3] This view needs modification. Cartier kidnapped Indians and used them to show to the French court that conversion of the heathen, with God's help, could be achieved. Moreover, slavery existed in New France, and did so either legally or illegally from 1632, when the first slave was sold in the colony, to 1760, when slavery was given new life under British law. Both *panis* (Indians) and Blacks were slaves in Canada and in 1760 there were some 4,000. The economy of the frontier, whether of the forest or the farm, required no gang labor of the slave or "indentured" type. There were no plantation crops or silver mines. Consequently, though the institution was

3. "The French and the Indians," in Howard Peckham and Charles Gibson, eds., *Attitudes of Colonial Powers toward the American Indian* (Salt Lake City: University of Utah Press, 1969), p. 61.

well established, slavery never developed in New France to the degree it did in some English or Spanish colonies of the New World.[4]

The French regarded Indians as souls for conversion. A visitor to Canada, Sieur de Cobes, wrote in 1608 that the Indians were "very brutish" in their manner of living "but they are beginning to become civilized and to take on our manners and our ways. They are easily instructed in the Christian religion and are not too opinionated in their Paganism, to the extent that if Preachers went down to them I believe that in a short time the whole country would give in to the Christian faith without being otherwise constrained, and that by this means the way would be opened in the whole of the remainder of America for the conquest of souls, which is greater than all the lands one could ever conquer." He foresaw that with this achievement French glory would be eternal in America.

French monarchs also realized the wisdom of establishing the Christian religion in New France. In 1603 for instance, Henry IV ordered de Monts to acquaint the Indians with the Christian faith and religion. The economic motive was theoretically to parallel that of the missionary; but it did not necessarily follow that the merchant monopolists gave as much attention to the religious requirements of the charters as the Court would have wished. Only after the Jesuits received adequate backing in Parisian aristocratic circles in the 1630s did missionary work really progress. The Jesuit techniques for assimilating and acculturating the Indian included learning native languages, providing hospital care, and building seminaries.

Another aspect of French behavior toward the Indian was that intermarriage had the unwritten sanction of Church and State. Champlain, who dreamed of a new nation of French and Indians "on equal footing, for a common aim," told the Indians at Quebec "our young men will marry your daughters, and we shall become one people." Marry they did—in Acadia, in Quebec, and in the Northwest. French-Indian marriages were common in the wilderness. *Coureur de-bois*, the fur traders, and voyageurs, the canoe men, took wives *au fashion du Nord*—in the fashion of the North. This resulted in the appearance of a half-breed, French-speaking culture. The

4. See Robin W. Winks, *The Blacks in Canada: A History* (New Haven and London: Yale University Press; and Montreal: McGill Queen's University Press, 1971), chap. 1.

Métis, as they are called, were in fact the "new nation" of the West. One can speculate as to why no such new race evolved in the English colonies. New England agriculture required segregation, not mutual assistance. Possibly the French were less concerned with the question of race than were the English; perhaps also the Catholic exhibited a greater zeal for saving the infidel than did the Protestant. Indeed, the Jesuits argued that the Indians must be Frenchified before becoming Christians and to do this French civilization had to "embrace" and "cherish" the Indian. This policy of white-native contact was mild by comparison to its English and Spanish counterparts. It established a pattern in Canadian ethnic history which has no distinct parallel in the United States or Latin America.

Commerce, Settlement, and the Frontier

Champlain, the Jesuits, and the French Court wanted more than just good relations with the Indians. And they sought to make Canada more than merely an outpost for the fur trade. They wanted to colonize the St. Lawrence Valley and thus make it a jewel in the French crown. They asked how this could be done when monopolists in the trade failed to keep their obligations of sending out settlers in order to protect the Indian trade.

The French government took this matter into consideration in 1627. In that year, Cardinal Richelieu, the chief minister to Louis XIII and a man dedicated to rivalling Spanish, Dutch, and English power by building up a strong marine and colonial system, established a company of 100 shareholders. Known as the Company of New France or One Hundred Associates, it possessed the fur trade monopoly for fifteen years. In return, it was required to establish over 4,000 settlers in Acadia and Canada in the same period, was held responsible for the costs of administration, and was compelled to support the clergy. The fact that the majority of associates were wealthy nobles indicates Richelieu's desire to keep the scheme out of the hands of merchants who hitherto had been interested in the fur trade to the neglect of settlement. The nobles could be expected to take a keen interest in land holding, and the prospects for the expansion of the Canadian population beyond the 100 souls of 1627 looked bright.

From the outset, however, Richelieu's design faced great problems. In May 1628 four ships with 400 settlers left for Quebec. Off Gaspé they were captured by an expedition led by David Kirke, an Englishman commissioned by Charles I to seize Canada and set up trade and plantations in the St. Lawrence region for a group of London merchants. Kirke then aided a Scottish project under Sir William Alexander to settle Port Royal, cut off the Associates' supply ships from France, and in July 1629, finally forced Champlain to surrender a Quebec that was on the point of starvation. Had the English captured Quebec a year earlier it seems possible that they might have kept Canada at peace in April 1629. King Charles found Canada a useful bargaining point to get the remainder of a dowry owed him, and, on the strength of Richelieu's diplomacy, France regained Quebec and Port Royal by the Treaty of Saint-Germain-en-Laye in 1632, and did so to the disappointment of English and Scottish commercial and colonizing interests. Kirke later became governor of Newfoundland where Sir George Calvert had founded a fledgling settlement at Avalon. Alexander never lived to see his Nova Scotia (New Scotland) become a reality. As for Champlain, he resumed command at Quebec in 1633, rebuilt the fortress, and died there in 1635.

To stimulate emigration from France the Company of New France, beginning in 1627, granted property *en seigneurie et fief* to landholders (*seigneurs*) who to their own advantage would settle it with colonists (*censitaires* or *habitants*). The aim was regulated land control for the purpose of stimulating colonization.

The seigneuries, long and narrow, extended in parallel lines back from the river. This geometric pattern would be repeated within a seigneury itself, with strips of land running parallel to the boundaries and divided into concession rows (*rangs*) with unceded lands in the hinterland. This allowed habitants a variety of soil conditions and access to the river for purposes of water supply, fishing, and transportation. The seigneuries varied in size but the state preferred smaller divisions because they prevented subdivisions and discouraged the building of great landed estates. The grants were not confined to laity. After 1663 the Ursulines, Suplicans, Récollets, the Bishop and Seminary of Quebec, and especially the Jesuits were awarded lands which, by 1780, totalled 26 percent of all seigneurial lands. This percentage may seem high but it was probably justifiable in view of the social services in education and hospitalization provided by the

Church. At the time of the British conquest in 1760, there were some 250 seigneuries containing nearly 8 million acres.

The seigneurial regime appears to have been hierarchical in nature and to have reflected the theoretical absolutism and paternalism of French colonial policy. On the other hand, it was not feudal: the seigneur was the king's land agent and not a liege lord. He had duties to perform within the law. He was bound to pay fealty and homage to the governor and to subject himself to the crown's inquiries. He could not sell his lands without paying a tax of a fifth of the selling price. To the habitant he had other duties. He was obliged to maintain a manor house, a step designed to prevent absentee landlordism. He was also required to cede lands to applicants, to operate a flour mill, to hold court, to support the church, and to do road work (*corvée*) with the *censitaires*. He had, of course, honors owing him and "burdensome rights" payable by the habitant. The latter, burdensome but not oppressive, were designed to discourage land transfer and keep the habitant on the soil. They were also intended to protect the habitant against seigneurial abuses and, in this connection, the habitant had rights of appeal to the intendant. The seigneurial regime, far from being feudal then, was actually a system of checks and balances designed for the mutual benefit of landlord and settler.

What was the role of environment—of the "frontier," if you wish—in the development of French colonial society in Canada at this time? The wilderness posed as an "escape valve" to those who sought to profit by the fur trade or to escape the pressures of urban or even agricultural society.[5] In France there was competition for land. In New France there was competition for labor. Indeed, to prevent too many young men from taking to the woods, the government instituted a system of licensing canoes and traders. By this method it was hoped habitants would be kept on the land, cultivating crops important to colonial self-sufficiency. But the habitant, Charlevoix wrote, "breathed from his birth the air of liberty" and the frontier offered freedoms. The fur trade that became increasingly profitable as the seventeenth century progressed drew habitants to the

5. The evidence is inconclusive that the society of New France totally reflected the frontier environment. Compare A. L. Burt, "The Frontier in the History of New France," *Canadian Historical Association Report, 1940* (Toronto, 1940), pp. 93–99, esp. p. 98; and W. J. Eccles, *The Canadian Frontier, 1534–1760* (New York: Holt, Rinehart and Winston, Inc., 1969), p. 216.

wilderness. In the forests, the flamboyant, gaudy *coureurs-de-bois* adopted Indian styles of living and frontier values. They thus concerned the colony's authorities, both civil and ecclesiastical.

Not only was the frontier an ameliorating feature on French institutions transported into Canada, it was the source of danger. In the mid-seventeenth century, the eyes of New France were fixed on the southern frontier, where the Iroquois threat reached decisive proportions. The French, allied with the Algonkins and Huron, were in bitter conflict with the Iroquois who traded with the Dutch at Fort Orange (Albany). Between 1640 and 1660 the Iroquois attacked French settlements along the St. Lawrence, intercepted furs coming downriver on the Ottawa, and terrorized the Jesuit missions and Indian villages in Huronia. The horrors of this war in terms of its effect on both Indian and Jesuit defy description. The Iroquois gained control of the western fur trade, their ultimate aim. As for the Hurons, they ceased to exist as a nation capable of waging war. Moreover, the Jesuits withdrew from Huronia and kept priests only at a few scattered and strategic points on the Great Lakes. The future of French empire in the West was therefore in question.

French power was equally in doubt in settled areas. Near the new towns of Montreal and Trois Rivières, founded in 1634 and 1642, respectively, Iroquois warriors took scalps with ease. This pressure reached a high point in 1660 but was relieved at Long Sault by Adam Dollard des Ormeaux, the garrison commander of Montreal, of Canadian legend. The Indian frontier was momentarily stabilized. Meanwhile, Acadia had fallen to Massachusetts expansionists. In 1654 a fleet from Boston captured Port Royal and Fort St. John and in 1662 an English governor was commissioned for the area. French power in North America, confined to the empire of the St. Lawrence, tottered ominously. Reports from Quebec—variously charged with emotion and fear and telling of the untapped prospects of the colony—reached Versailles. Their message was direct: the fate of New France was sealed unless France would send support. The frontier would have to be held by force.

The Crown Colony: Its Rise and Fall

The French Crown heard these clear and desperate appeals for assistance. In March 1661, following the death of the dominating Cardinal Mazaran, the young Louis XIV had dramatically assumed control of affairs with the ambition of making France the strongest European power. The Sun King's minister, the great mercantilist Jean-Baptiste Colbert, had similar intentions. He knew that a strong navy and colonies were necessary for the rise of French national power. They reorganized colonial administration and in 1665 created the Ministry of Marine, which directed colonial and naval finances and administration. Colbert, as Minister of Marine, now dictated affairs of the French empire as he and his monarch wished.

In May 1663 the king decreed that New France was to be, like the king's other possessions at home, a royal province. At the same time, the charter of the defunct Company of New France was cancelled and with it the fur-trade monopoly. Chartered companies were founded to develop French interests in such places as San Domingo and Louisiana; and in Canada a crown corporation, the *Compagnie de l'Occident,* founded in 1664, was a means of infusing royal control and monies into the colony. The Crown assumed responsibility for the administration and defense of the colony.

The new regime called for the establishing of a sovereign or superior council. This would consist of a governor, responsible for relations with the French administration and for defense of the colony; an intendant, responsible for the justice, economy, police, and finance of the colony; and a bishop, responsible for ecclesiastical affairs (and, at his own discretion, moral guardianship). Other council members included an attorney-general, a clerk of the records, and five councillors, usually representing the merchant class. The resulting conciliar government was rife with conflicts. Yet periodically it gave the colony the local direction lacking under full company auspices. Certainly, the personality and character of the individuals holding office were reflected in the colonial administration; and periodically, graft worked assiduously to the disadvantage of the colony's military preparedness. But the coming of royal government to Canada marked the end of the era: new government institutions, designed to reshape New France in the image of the old world, were to change forever the social fabric of the colony.

The French government saw that the immediate need of the colony in 1663 was protection from the Iroquois. Several companies of troops, including the famous Carignan-Salières regiment of some 1,100 men, were dispatched to Quebec after 1665. They first erected several forts on the southern frontier. Then, in a series of raids and displays of power led by Governor Courcelle, and the Marquis de Tracy, the army checked the Mohawk danger. They put four Mohawk villages to the torch, destroyed food supplies, and erected a large cross and a post bearing the French arms at the site of the principal village. They were establishing a *cordon sanitaire*. In July 1667, the Iroquois Confederacy was compelled to treat with the French at Quebec. This ended their hostilities with both the French and Algonkians until 1682. As for the soldiers, about 400 officers and men remained at the end of their tour of duty to settle near Montreal and the Richelieu River and form the core of a militia established in 1673 and responsible for the defense of that vulnerable back door to Canada. Elsewhere in the colony, militia captains, chosen from the habitants, assumed responsibility for local defense.

The resident royal bureaucracy undertook numerous steps to make the colony self-supporting and populous. When the great Jean Talon was commissioned intendant of all French possessions in North America in 1665, the colony had only some 3,000 residents. He would have to satisfy Colbert's demand that Canada be self-sufficient and thus develop adequate agriculture, trade, and industry. He encouraged experimentation in crop production, brewing, and shipbuilding. He also took steps to people the country. From 1665 to 1672, about 1,500 state-aided immigrants and indentured employees landed in Canada and were given land, implements, and supplies. Some 900 *filles de roi* or "king's daughters," orphans raised by nuns at the crown's expense, were imported as wives for the soldiers. It is reported that the "fattest went off best, upon the apprehension that these being less active, would keep truer to their Ingagements, and hold out better against the nipping cold of the Winter." The Crown also sent some 1,000 criminals, mainly poachers and salt smugglers, in the eighteenth century. In 1668 a ship arrived with Portuguese, German, and Dutch settlers. Huguenots, though generally debarred, came to New France intermittently, where they caused the bishop concern. Talon, on Colbert's advise, issued regulations to encourage early marriages and large families. He also imposed heavy penalties on reluctant bachelors and fathers of would-be brides. The very Canadian system of baby bonus and family allowance was born. The Church also encouraged marriage: marriage beds were blessed and exorcised, and the betrothed well understood that the chief purpose of matrimonial state was procreation.

In the family-centered society of New France marriage was a popular state. Widows and widowers frequently remarried; few women went into holy orders; illegitimacy was low. The family was engaged in a collective enterprise for survival, self-sufficiency, and upward advancement, and marriages were invariably contractual arrangements in which large dowries were significant. In this healthy and productive society low infant mortality rates existed: twice the population reached marriageable age in New than in Old France.

All these factors resulted in phenomenal population growth. In the period from 1666 to 1673, the population doubed from 3,200 to 6,700. By 1713 it was 18,000; by 1730, 34,000; and at the conquest, 76,000. This amazing growth was almost wholly indigenous: only 10,000 emigrated from Europe during the whole French colonial period. Of these, the composition was 3,500 soldiers, 1,100 girls, 3,900 indentured workers, 500 independent males, 1,000 condemned criminals.[6] Colbert did not want to populate New France at the expense of Old France, and French immigration to the New World was a trifling portion of that of the English. Nonetheless, for the reasons given, the French-Canadians experienced a fecundity that numbered them 340,000 in 1820, 650,000 in 1850, and 6.5 million in 1970.

As the population grew in the early years of the eighteenth century, the economy advanced. Bridges and canals were built. New seigneuries were granted and a few ships laid down, ironworks founded, and fishing and sealing occupied a few colonists. However, in none of these occupations was there significant economic expansion. Why? The reason for this has been well explained by Marcel Trudel:

> When Champlain sketched out a program of development in 1618, he had set a value of some 3,600,000 *livres* per year on the possible income from fisheries and mines, and from wood and wood products, hemp, canvas, and rope manufacturing. However, during the first half of the seventeenth century, the mother country was still only

6. Jean Hamelin, *Economie et société en Nouvelle-France* (Québec, 1960), pp. 76–100; also W. J. Eccles, *France in America* (New York; Harper and Row, 1972), p. 72.

> interested in furs. Then, under Colbert, nothing was considered "more important for the expansion of this colony than the search for merchandise and the establishing of mills and fisheries." Intendant Talon became the enthusiastic agent of this policy, but unfortunately, the policies of the mother country were soon to restrict industry to the immediate and essential needs of the colony. For example, in 1704, the King prohibited the making of canvas in Canada at the expense of the French product. The theory behind this action was that "nothing that might compete with the manufactured goods of this Kingdom must ever be made in the colonies." The colonies existed solely to supply raw materials and were only being maintained "for the benefit of the countries which founded them and never with the intention of dispensing with those countries." This view was to be the standard French policy. When the manufacture of beaver hats was begun in Montreal and Quebec, the mother country gave strict orders, in 1736, to close down the factories. Hatmaking could have become the starting point for a rich industrial life.
>
> Under these conditions, permission was granted only to industries satisfying the essential needs of the country: shipbuilding and ironworks, fisheries, and the products of small-scale industry.[7]

In other words, French mercantilism aimed at colonial self-sufficiency, which was not to be at the expense of the metropolitan power. For this reason New France remained essentially a colony in which fur was the most important article of trade.

Put another way, because New France did not have a flourishing commerce with the outside world, its society reflected its basic dependence on the fur staple. Elsewhere within the empire, in the Lesser Antilles (St. Christopher, Guadeloupe, and Martinique) and in Cayenne on the Guiana coast, the French were less vigorous in colonizing than were the English. Capital, leadership, and entrepreneurs were scarce.

Thus, while New France produced various agricultural products for trade on the fishing banks, at Cape Breton and in the French West Indies, while it had a seemingly inexhaustible fishing ground, and while it had excellent forests and mineral reserves, it lacked—in

7. *Introduction to New France* (Toronto and Montreal: Holt, Rinehart and Winston of Canada, Ltd., 1968), p. 199. Reprinted by permission of Holt, Rinehart and Winston of Canada, Limited.

its dependent position—a society capable of exploiting that potential. It was easy to blame management. As one memorialist wrote to the Regent of France in 1715, "This vast stretch of country is immensely wealthy . . . but restricting ourselves only to those areas actually inhabited by Frenchmen, and of the Gulf and Saint Lawrence River linked to the trade with the indigenous inhabitants, we can easily conclude that if the affairs of the country are in poor condition it is not due to the nature of the land, but rather to the poor management of those who have directed the colony."

In these circumstances, it is not surprising that French colonial society in Canada did not flourish to the degree of its English counterparts. The basic paternalistic structure of government—both in the colony and in the relationship to the home government—denied the development of an expansive commercial and industrial society. New France had bankers, merchants, and entrepreneurs, but the way of life in the colony was more typified by *habitants* and *coureurs-de-bois.* The colony was stifled by economic regulation and frequently riddled with graft and corruption.

In its spiritual and intellectual growth, its society remained within confines defined by clergy and crown. Books were of French rather than local manufacture. There is no record of a printing press in New France and there was no book trade. The grand sum of books in the colony was probably 20,000; and of these, religious works were in the majority. New France had no public library.

In education, as well, growth was slow. Various religious orders kept schools. Many but not all parishes had a *petite école* but illiteracy remained extensive. Quebec and Montreal each had a trade school. In 1635 the Jesuits established a college in Quebec for the purpose of preparing students to be priests, navigators, and surveyors. Students of medicine or the law were trained in France. Local cultural developments were not entirely lacking. New France had its men of science and letters, its wood sculptors, silversmiths, and painters, its musicians and actors. But the French enlightenment had few effusions on the west side of the Atlantic. And, as the eighteenth century progressed, the intellectual gap between Old and New France widened.

Unlike the English-American colonies with their wealthy middle class and year-round connections with the British Isles and elsewhere,

New France, with its society of essentially needy lower-class origin, had a limited intellectual life. The French colonist possessed a social ethic quite different from that of his New England Protestant counterpart. Born of different linguistic and religious stock, living under different institutions of land control and authoritarian government, he developed a unique posture concerning his earth, *terre Quebec*. The French-Canadian adopted no "puritanical" outlook in the American sense. Yet he came under close Jesuit surveillance, for church codes of social behavior were by no means lacking in Canada in the late seventeenth century. His attitude toward the North American Indian contrasted with that of his English or Spanish counterpart. As an *emigré* of France he tended to be of rural, military, or clerical background. His colonial attitudes underwent little change. By contrast, those of his Massachusetts or Virginia counterparts were nurtured by changing economic and political conditions and hence developed revolutionary overtones and expansionistic tendencies at a much faster rate.

French-Canadian society, rooted in land and Catholicism, was not outward-looking. Rather it had the deficiencies of an unnurtured society far from metropolitan France. Be that as it may, French-Canadian society was of such stability and tradition that its legacies remained well after the British conquest.

In the last analysis, however, the fate of New France was not determined by the characteristics of the populace or economy but by the state of international relations and British naval and military paramountcy. Four wars—beginning in 1689 and ending in 1763—were fought by France and England; and the end result in North America, as signified by the Treaty of Paris of 1763, was that the French empire there was at an end. Only the islands St. Pierre and Miquelon, off the south Newfoundland coast, remained French, as shelters and drying places for French fishermen.

French imperial efforts of no small merit had failed to hold the colony. The colonization at New Orleans in 1718 and the building of the great fortress port of Louisbourg at Cape Breton in 1720 to secure both ends of a vast and fragile network of forts along the great interconnecting empires of the St. Lawrence and the Mississippi had not been enough. The growth of English settlement in New England, New York, and the middle colonies was a force that threatened

French settlements both in Acadia and, in time, on the banks of the St. Lawrence. In 1760 Canada had 76,000 colonists as compared with the Thirteen Colonies' 1,599,000. On the shores of Hudson Bay, also, the vigorous growth of the English fur trade under Hudson's Bay Company auspices after 1668 (ironically with the know-how of the *coureurs* Radisson and Groseilliers) threatened the interior appendages of trade of empire of the St. Lawrence. The British victory at Quebec on September 13, 1759 was but a climax to an ongoing process which historians have called the Second Hundred Years' Wars.

Geographical facts and British sea hegemony had told the tale: New France, confined to the great river and unable to be assisted from overseas, now became a British province in a North American empire stretching from the Arctic Islands to the Gulf of Mexico and from the Atlantic shore to the Mississippi. Its extent to the north and west of the Great Lakes had yet to be defined. The continuance of French-Canadian race and culture would depend very largely on the deep roots of its colonial society and on the new order of British rule.

"The ties with the mother country," Hilda Neatby has written, "so much more and completely a mother than Britain had been to any of her active and sometimes ungainly offspring, were severed. One more journey direct to France could be taken, by British permission in a British ship, and then no more except by special permit from London and London officials, separated from the Canadians on the St. Lawrence by many barriers of which language was only one." [8] It was somewhat characteristic of the remote, paternalistic, and to some degree primitive society of Quebec that Canon Briand, the grand vicar of Quebec, ordered prayers to be said for the new king of the province, George III, and this in advance of the formal recognition of British sovereignty in the Treaty of Paris. In Briand's opinion the British "are our masters; and we owe to them what we owed to the French when they ruled." Thus, the kingdom of Canada passed from the hands of one European power to another.

8. *Quebec, The Revolutionary Age 1760–1791* (Toronto and Montreal: McClelland and Stewart, Ltd., 1966), p. 3.

3

Colonial Identities in Transformation

The period 1763 to 1867 witnessed the emergence or modification of several colonial identities in British America. These included French-Canadians (*Canadiens*) who now had to observe the sovereignty of the British Crown and the regulations of British mercantilism; Upper Canadians who were in the main born of the American Revolution and antipathetic to its principles; Maritime colonists who owed their existence to, yet were divided by, the sea; Red River settlers whose blood reflected their varied ethnic heritages; and British Columbians whose mountainous or maritime existence in a remote quarter of the Empire gave them a unique perspective. British America in 1867 was as diverse in its peoples as it was in its geography. And yet there were certain common denominators—in Crown and parliamentary institutions, in law and authority, in defense and commerce, in symbols and ideas, and in opposition to American expansion and republicanism—that gave these sprawling locales a certain unity or common basis, if a precarious one. Indians and Eskimos became increasingly dependent as colonization advanced.

Colonial Identities in Empire and Revolution

One of these limited identities was that of the French-Canadians. After the conquest, their ties with France by commerce and immigration terminated, as did the fur trade with the continental interior. With London displacing Paris as the metropolitan center of empire, the *Canadiens* were now shut off from old roots and opportunities.[1] War had brought an end to the French connection and an Indian-European conflict, commonly though mistakenly known as Pontiac's "rebellion," created turbulence on the western frontier of trade. In this new colonial system both *Canadiens* and Indians were subject peoples, and the British, in a well-known policy arrangement called the Proclamation of 1763, defined the new colonial context.

This colonial administrative plan was intended to regulate both *Canadien* and Indian affairs. It established English law throughout the province of Quebec and through supplementary regulation the governor could grant Crown lands freehold, though actually French civil law and the seigneurial regime were to remain in existence. It also stated that the province, like its counterparts in the Thirteen Colonies, East and West Florida, and the British West Indies, was to have an assembly, though this was only a promise. Power would reside in the governor and council. These manifestations of imperial policy reflect the assumption that British subjects would migrate to the St. Lawrence lowlands from Britain or the Empire in sufficient numbers that in time the province would become English-speaking. But historical developments, especially the American Revolution, and demographic facts, especially the growing *canadien* populace, were to preclude this. With regard to Indian relations the so-called Proclamation Line along the watershed of the Allegheny Mountains from north to south divided, in theory at least, lands of British settle-

1. The literature on *Canadiens* in the period 1763 to 1867 is voluminous and growing. The question of *canadien* decapitation and of *bourgeois* collapse is a matter of controversy and ongoing economic and social research. Some sources for further study are: Fernand Ouellet, *Histoire économique et sociale du Québec, 1760–1850* (Montreal and Paris: Fides, 1966; English translation, Carleton Library); Jean-Pierre Wallot, "Le régime seigneurial et son abolition au Canada," *Canadian Historical Review,* 50 (December 1969), 367–93; Alfred Dubuc, "Problems in the Study of the Stratification of the Canadian Society from 1760 to 1840," Canadian Historical Association, *Report,* 1965, pp. 13–29 (reprinted in Michiel Horn and Ronald Sabourin, *Studies in Canadian Social History* [Toronto: McClelland and Stewart, Ltd., 1974), pp. 123–39]); R. Cole Harris and John Warkentin, *Canada Before Confederation: An Historical Geography* (New York: Oxford University Press, 1974), pp. 65–109; and Hilda Neatby, *Quebec: The Revolutionary Age, 1760–1791* (Toronto: McClelland and Stewart, Ltd., 1966).

ment from a vast Indian preserve where European settlement was disallowed but trade could be conducted by government license. London's intention was to protect the Indian from frontier settlement, allow time for a more permanent arrangement with regard to the disposal of Indian lands and regulation of trade in the Ohio Valley and Great Lakes region, and deflect American settlement northward, as in Nova Scotia's case, to Quebec.

The creation of the "Indian Territory" had important implications for the *Canadiens*. This had been their frontier of westward expansion and one of their contacts with the outer world. Now an arbitrary line cut them off politically from age-old trading and military allies—the Ottawas, Senecas, Huron, Chippewas, and others—who had come to the great French forts of an earlier day—Michilimackinac, Detroit, and Niagara. In short, Quebec was truncated on the west and its relationship with Europe was thus transformed. Small wonder that in the years of British rule after 1763 its society was bound to fold inward, with continuing consequences for our own times.

The whole world of *canadien* society now became the protracted space between the Appalachian Mountains and the Canadian Shield. And in that area, although the *canadien* population grew rapidly at the rate of 55 per thousand per year and by 1861 numbered 850,000 French-speaking persons (whereas in 1760 there had been 76,000), the English seemed everywhere in the ascendant. The latter and their collaborators dominated wealth, foreign and domestic trade, patronage and executive positions in government and business. They filled or displaced the French or *canadien* political, administrative, social, and political elite, 2,000 in all, who left the colony shortly after 1760. They acquired seigneurial and freehold lands, let contracts for public works to each other, gave appointments to their own kind, and dominated commerce and industry while the *Canadiens* drew together as a closely knit, self-aware, rural minority within the British Empire and North America. French-speaking seigneurs and clergy in positions of influence transferred allegiance to their new masters with little trouble, but the overall implications for the *Canadiens* and Indians under the new order in northern North America was extensive. British bayonets in Montreal and Michilimackinac had a decisive psychological impact on Gallic and Amerind races alike. These new subjects of

"His Britannic Majesty" would continue for centuries to live with the legacies of this transformation.

The British intended that Quebec should be anglicized. Governor James Murray, an officer who had served with Wolfe at Quebec, had instructions to govern with a twelve-man council, none of whom could be Catholic under terms of the Elizabethan Test Act. He was to encourage the work of Protestant churches and schools in Quebec and was not to permit any ecclesiastical jurisdiction by Rome. He soon learned, however, that the *Canadiens* had no desire to be assimilated. Nor were they "swamped" by British immigrants, as the government had assumed would be the case. British subjects did not settle in the St. Lawrence lowlands in great numbers. The result was that Murray had to govern under other than expected circumstances. He kept at heel 600 British merchants—Americans, English, and Scots—who through petition to London frantically sought an assembly and local political control. His sympathies for the *Canadiens* are noteworthy. He believed them to be "perhaps the bravest and best race upon the globe," and he believed that if they were relieved of their political handicaps as Roman Catholics they would soon become "the most faithful and most useful set of men in this American empire." But these views were not appreciated by British patriots of Montreal, Trois Rivières, and Quebec and in 1766 Murray was recalled to face charges brought forth by the merchants to the effect that he had exhibited tyranny and partiality. However, at the hearing the charges were dismissed for lack of evidence.

Murray was succeeded by another army officer who had served with Wolfe, Sir Guy Carleton (later Lord Dorchester). Carleton continued Murray's policy of conciliation. He likewise believed that an assembly was impracticable, and it was his forceful arguments in the period 1770 to 1774 that convinced the British government to suspend the idea of representative government as proclaimed in 1765 and instead, to maintain the system of governor and appointed council.

These policies were outlined in the Quebec Act of 1774. In addition to its provisions regarding the form of government, already mentioned, the Act restored to Quebec the Indian lands of the middle West as far as the junction of the Ohio and Mississippi Rivers. This adjustment attached the fur area of the continental interior to its natural outlet and seat of government regulation at Quebec. To the east, the colony's boundaries now included Labrador, Anticosti Island, and the Magdalen Islands in the Gulf of St. Lawrence. They also extended northward to the boundaries of the Hudson's Bay Company territory of Rupert's Land.

The Quebec Act provided that English law would continue as the colony's criminal law. But French civil law was reestablished, and this meant that land tenure including seigneuries, marriage, inheritance, trade, and commerce remained undisturbed. Perhaps most important, Catholics could hold office upon swearing an oath of allegiance which was made inoffensive to them and to the Protestants. As for the Catholic clergy, it was given the right of collecting church tithes. Finally, the administrative costs of the colony were to be met by terms of the Quebec Revenue Act. This system of indirect taxes and customs duties was not an onerous levy; to cite one example, no direct taxes were placed on beer—only on tavern keepers.

Most of this was the work of Carleton, who had believed that Quebec would continue as French-speaking and Catholic to be the bastion of the old order in a New World seething with democracy. He had done his part to insure that the old institutions of New France were left intact and did so in an era of the gathering storm that resulted in the American Revolution. His contribution to the preservation of *canadien* institutions is greater than some of the critics of his "paternal despotism" are prepared to admit.

But embittered American colonists did not see Carleton's Quebec Act as beneficial. Instead, they listed it as one of the so-called "Intolerable Acts," whose aim was to control the older American colonies. They argued that it did not provide for an assembly, that it entrenched "popery" on the banks of the St. Lawrence, and that it extended the boundaries of Quebec in a southwesterly direction so as to interfere with the ancient trans-Appalachian claims of some of their own colonies. Further, they regarded it as a sinister British plot to threaten their democracy and as a military means to weaken their cause. Thus, imbued with friendliness toward the *Canadiens* and hatred toward George III and Parliament, the first Continental Congress, in September 1774, passed the following resolution initiated by Massachusetts: "The late Act of Parliament for establishing the Roman Catholic religion and the French laws in that extensive country now called Canada is dangerous in an extreme degree to the Protestant religion and to the civil rights and liberties of all America: and therefore, as men and Protestant Christians, we are indispensably obliged to take all proper measures to protect our safety." Congress invited the French-Canadians to join in a social compact under the "generous principles of equal liberty."

Because the citizens of Quebec did not rise against the British government, the Americans assumed the stance as liberators. They sent agents to Quebec to get support for the Revolution; they found this support among certain British-Americans who Carleton knew were known "to forward sedition and applaud rebellion." These agents were unsuccessful.

Why did the *Canadiens* not join the Revolution? For one thing, British military might in the great garrison at Quebec could not be overthrown. For another, the American invasion of 1775 was poorly executed. Finally, the *Canadiens* did not rise against the British, as the Americans had expected. The Quebec Act had not coerced the *Canadiens;* seigneurs, clergy, and habitants had been unmolested since 1763 and preferred the status quo. Though some habitants had helped the invaders from the beginning, many were alienated from "les Yankis" when they received payment for supplies in useless currency or notes. The American general Wooster's decision to prohibit the holding of mass in a Montreal church on Christmas eve, 1775 similarly alienated the *Canadiens.* Quebec and the *Canadiens* had not joined the Revolution. It can be speculated that had Canada been populated by the English for as long as Massachusetts or Virginia, rebellion might have spread and Canada become American. Paradoxically, Canada remained British because its inhabitants were French.

Nova Scotia colonists also rejected revolution, but unlike the Quebec case, theirs was an instance of how a region on the fringes of the Revolution was torn by conflicting forces, and in the end remained passively neutral. Of the seventeen or eighteen thousand settlers, three-quarters were New Englanders by birth. But though they knew of the complaints across the waters in Boston and Philadelphia and had close family ties there, they were part of the British colonial system of mercantilism. In Halifax, the capital, a cautious oligarchy maintained close ties with London merchants, and this same group maintained a dominance in the provincial assembly at the expense of rural areas. They looked on the war as advantageous for war contracts and good for trade. And, with the naval base for Royal Navy ships in the North Atlantic and Caribbean situated in Bedford Basin adjacent to Halifax, how could a revolution be got up anyway? It was only in the out-settlements such as in Cumberland county that the fervors of revolution ran high. Outbursts against the Crown did occur and indicated the sympathies of the rural or outport majority. But as the Revolution progressed, the Nova Scotians found themselves cut off by sea from their former New England homelands, and they were divided one from another by the roadless Nova Scotian wilderness. Occasionally Yankee ships made raids on the coastal ports and this tended to weaken pro-revolutionary support. Thus, somewhat ironically, the Yankees who had conquered Acadia and expelled the Acadians now found themselves torn between revolutionary and reactionary forces. In the end, they became, as one historian called them, "The Neutral Yankees of Nova Scotia." [2]

The Treaty of Versailles of 1783 brought peace in this civil war of English-speaking peoples with differing imperial, commercial, and continental ambitions. The North American/Anglo-American empire in existence since the Proclamation of 1763 had been succeeded by republican nationalists in the South and British colonists in the North.

North of the new border, the American Revolution left long-standing political and psychological legacies. For British-Americans, empire was the guardian of liberty, their protection from the American republicanism they abhorred. Union Jack and Crown, British gunboats and garrisons were symbols of security in a continent where republicanism seemed to them to be in the ascendant. The Duke of Wellington regarded Canada as "all frontier and nothing else" and behind that frontier on the Canadian side, the inhabitants developed myths about cultural superiority but could not avoid the reality that again the border might be crossed by American invaders.

The political frontier that separated them from their rivals after

2. John Bartlett Brebner, *The Neutral Yankees of Nova Scotia: A Marginal Colony during the Revolutionary Years* (New York: Columbia University Press, 1937).

1783 gave some recognition to the geographical integrity of the St. Lawrence below the Richelieu River. But it divided the Champlain basin tributary to the great river. More significantly, in the West it failed to include the middle West to the junction of the Ohio and Mississippi as recognized in the Quebec Act, and instead, ran through the Great Lakes and to the Lake of the Woods. The British, more concerned with trade than dominion, seem to have paid no attention to what British and Montreal merchants and their Indian allies opposed—that is, the abandoning of the great Southwestern plan of Empire first devised by La Salle. The boundary followed the middle of the St. Lawrence south and west of the 45th parallel, through the middle of the Great Lakes, along the Rainy River to the northwest corner of the Lake of the Woods, and then due west to where the Mississippi River was thought to be found—mistakenly, as it was proved. By this the key trading posts of the interior, including Oswego, Niagara, Detroit, and Michilimackinac, were abandoned to the Americans. The British negotiators had given way to American aspirations of westward expansion. They had likewise sacrificed the geographical integrity of the St. Lawrence and with it the ancient commercial system of Montreal extending in a natural direction south and west to the Ohio country. This first case of sacrifice of Canadian colonial interests and territorial claims for reasons of facilitating Anglo-American accord and trade was a theme often to be repeated in Canadian history, and was to be in its own right a certain driving force behind Canadian nationalism.

Yet in spite of these territorial "giveaways," it must be remembered that British negotiators did not accede to American demands that Canada be surrendered. They were unprepared to sacrifice that portion of North America that had been held by British arms. Labrador, Newfoundland, Nova Scotia, Quebec, and Rupert's Land still bulked large on maps of North America.

The American Revolution induced major migrations to British America, which strengthened pro-empire sentiment while at the same time adding American social and cultural mores to the emerging mosaic north of the border. The Revolution was in many ways a civil war, and the success of the patriot cause in the Thirteen Colonies brought persecution, humiliation, anticonspiracy committees, fines, confiscations, death, test laws, and oaths of allegiance—all designed to make patriots out of Loyalists. As one evacuee put it, "Neither Hell, Hull nor Halifax can afford worse shelter than Boston."

During and after the war, banishment or voluntary exile was the experience of about 100,000 American Tories. Some 40,000, among the first of many displaced persons to find their way to Canada as a result of political upheavals elsewhere, made their way into British North America. About 10,000 of them—of all classes—went to the vacant lands of the St. John River Valley of Nova Scotia. This place and its environs they mockingly called "Nova Scarcity," and this area became a separate colony under the name of New Brunswick in 1784, with its own governor, legislature, and judiciary. Other Loyalists settled in southern Nova Scotia, Cape Breton Island, and Prince Edward Island. Nantucket whalers, more interested in economics than politics, located in Dartmouth, Nova Scotia, to benefit from British mercantile regulations for encouraging the southern whale fishery.

A further 10,000 Loyalists crossed into Canada to settle the Niagara peninsula, the St. Clair River region, and various townships and land grants in what was then southwestern Quebec. These new colonists, mostly from New York and Vermont, sought an outlet for political liberties they had enjoyed in the American colonies. They wanted their own assembly, separation of their freehold lands from the seigneuries, and complete freehold land tenure. They encouraged relatives and friends to come from the United States and by 1791 there were about 25,000 people living in southern Ontario. By 1812 their number had risen to about 90,000, of whom 20 percent could be classified as "Loyalists," 60 percent as "non-Loyalist Americans" (the "late Loyalists" of various ethnic extractions), and 20 percent as "other." The Loyalists brought slaves with them to Canada but within two decades of the Revolution had begun to equate slavery with the republic they had left, and soon began to end the practice and develop movements for abolition. The institution was terminated by statute in Upper Canada in 1793.

The migration of Loyalists also made constitutional change in the Province of Quebec inevitable: new institutions of Church and State were essential to accommodate the desires of both English- and French-speaking subjects, whether Protestant or Catholic. The British government believed that a properly balanced form of government with strong executive powers and with provisions for conciliar government and assemblies in Quebec would keep the colonists happy and insure the continuance of British institutions.

These principles were reflected in the Constitutional (or Canada) Act of 1791. It divided Quebec into Upper and Lower Canada along the old seigneurial limits, with both the Island of Montreal and a portion of what might otherwise be southeastern Ontario west of the Ottawa River allocated to Lower Canada. The Act allowed each of the Canadas a lieutenant-governor with powers of veto, a council composed of members appointed for life, and an assembly. It also allowed for the reservation of lands in Upper Canada on the following proportions: one-seventh to be held for the Protestant clergy and a like amount for support of the governor and colonial administration. Land tenure was to be freehold in Upper Canada and either freehold or leasehold in Lower Canada. A landed aristocracy was to come into being but never did; the mind boggles at the thought of such persons as the Duke of Niagara Falls or the Marquis of Trois Rivières in a land of primitive frontier conditions, but that was Whitehall's intention in that counterrevolutionary age, and it was a theme taken up by the Upper Canadian colonial oligarchy which had its seat of power at York (after 1834 the town resumed its old name of Toronto).

What longstanding consequences did the Act have? For one thing, it allowed local differences and governments in the Canadas while simultaneously maintaining strong executive powers. Some of the colonial governors agreed with this policy. Colonel John Graves Simcoe of Upper Canada, for instance, wanted (but did not succeed in every particular) to make colonial society the mirror of British society and Upper Canada the bulwark of British North America. His counterparts in Lower Canada were similarly inclined, though they faced racial and religious obstacles that made more complex the attempts at anglicization. Governor Sir James Craig, for instance, met deep-rooted *canadien* social institutions and an emerging *canadien* nationalism which was not dissimilar to its Irish counterpart of that era. The Canada Act, as will be seen later, promoted oligarchies and the result alienated the populace in both the Canadas. Yet it kept the colonies from revolution and even union with the United

States, and it did much to mould the social fabric and thus the mentalities of the two colonies.

The War of 1812 and Its Aftermath

The imperial-colonial relationship and the various British-American colonial identities were further strengthened by war. After the American Revolution, relations between Britain and the United States continued on shaky ground. Some Americans who believed that the only answer was to control Canada repeated statements similar to George Washington's prediction of 1778: "if that country [Canada] is not with us, it will . . . be at least a troublesome if not a dangerous enemy to us."

In addition to the question of security, American politicians found irritating the commercial ambitions of the empire of the St. Lawrence south of the boundary. Loyalist claims for compensation were not being paid by the United States, and consequently Britain kept control of the southwestern posts until Jay's Treaty of 1794. This agreement ceded the posts to the Americans but allowed Canadian commerce south of the line to continue. The Indians in such areas as the Wabash Valley, who had nothing to say in these matters, tried to keep up the Canadian trade and to resist the encroachment of American settlers. The Battle of Tippecanoe (1811) in which Tecumseh, his brother "The Prophet," and others were to die in the Shawnee cause marked the decline of the Canadian-Indian trading alliance and the rise of American military influence in the Indiana Territory. American politicians then looked for a permanent solution to the interrelated questions of Canadian trade with such tribes as the Shawnee and of land control in the Midwest. The Americans also objected to British treatment of American ships, commerce, and seamen and British political activities in Florida and Texas. The result was that expansionists, both in and out of Congress, sought a military campaign that would strengthen their position in relation to Great Britain. Why not invade Canada, they argued, expel the British from the continent, and make the United States safe, peaceful, and secure?

In deciding to send an army to invade Canada in 1812 the American Congress had underestimated both British power in North America and British determination not to abandon their North American colonies to the Americans. Congress believed, foolishly, that the Ontario peninsula, so heavily populated with American settlers, would be an easy conquest, or, as Thomas Jefferson put it, "a mere matter of marching."

To Canadians and Americans alike, the War of 1812 was a renewal of an old encounter, and most theaters of war were familiar ones—the Atlantic Seaboard, the Great Lakes, and Louisiana. In the Atlantic, despite the early frigate victories that left the American public reeling with success, the British navy acquired command of the sea and by 1813 had enforced a blockade of the coast from Boston to New Orleans. Now the British could press their advantage and in 1813 they gave convoy support to a North West Company expedition to secure the far western fur trade at the mouth of the Columbia, where Americans had been since 1811. The coastal blockade meant that the Americans would have to attack the British at inland points, and they determined to undertake a three-pronged, simultaneous attack on Canada. By the Champlain-Richelieu access, by the Niagara Peninsula, and by Detroit, the American army was to attack and then march on Montreal and Quebec. But the British and Canadians enjoyed a high degree of success on the battlefield. Control of the lakes was sometimes in doubt but never the total control of the Ontario peninsula. The brilliant feats of General Sir Isaac Brock at Queenstown Heights had other parallels along the Canadian border. At the same time, the ill-trained, badly led American forces suffered some embarrassing defeats. Only at New Orleans, where 10,000 British veterans of European campaigns led by Sir Edward Pakenham were repulsed by Andrew Jackson and his frontiersmen in January 1815, did Americans enjoy a splendid victory. Even so, in the irony of circumstances, the battle had occurred fifteen days after the Peace of Ghent had been signed in Belgium.

The war begun for control of North America ended in the maintenance of the *status quo ante bellum*. The Peace failed to resolve the maritime rights question or make a western boundary. But it did allow that a joint commission would resolve several issues including the boundary from the Saint Croix River to the Lake of the Woods, the question of British navigation of the Mississippi, and American rights to fish. Subsequently, the Convention of 1818 provided for a boundary along the 49th parallel from the Lake of the Woods to the Rocky Mountains. The New Brunswick–Maine boundary controversy was not considered, but that of Oregon was discussed and there joint control agreed on. On the fisheries question, the Americans were barred from the in-shore fisheries of the British colonies.

Canadians, unlike the Americans, did not view the War of 1812 as an exercise in frustration or an unsuccessful military venture. They regarded it as a great victory for themselves and for the British Empire. More important, the war colored their basic outlook toward the American republic. Loyalists became Canadians. As John Beverley Robinson, the Chief Justice of Upper Canada claimed, the war "produced in the British colonists a national character and feeling." Robinson and his contemporaries believed that henceforth they would have to fight "a constant struggle for independence against a powerful and unprincipled neighbour." The result was that the Upper Canada Tory governing class employed every means of "state, church, and school to control immigration, check loyalty, ferret out treason, and inculcate the right values." [3] Canadians now began to realize that British North America was not "a kind of subarctic, second-best America, but rather a genuine alternative to this revolution-born democracy, and organized upon principles quite different from it." [4]

Another longstanding effect of the War of 1812 was that both British and United States governments shared a suspicion of the rival's activities in the period 1815 to 1871. Although the Rush-Bagot naval agreement of 1817 limited armed vessels, tonnage, and armaments on the Great Lakes, its provisions were frequently violated by both parties. War clouds gathered during the Oregon boundary controversy in 1844–1846; the San Juan Island dispute, 1859–1860; the United States Civil War, 1861–1865; and the Fenian scares of the 1860s. In British North America the British maintained large garrisons, settled areas for strategic reasons, enlarged militias, and built canals such as the Rideau and Lachine with strategic and commercial considerations in mind. They strengthened forts or naval bases at Montreal, Lake Champlain, Kingston, and elsewhere. They built the huge military

3. S. F. Wise, in Wise and Robert Craig Brown, *Canada Views the United States: Nineteenth-Century Political Attitudes* (Seattle and London: University of Washington Press, 1967), p. 42.

4. *Ibid.*, p. 22.

stronghold at Quebec after 1823 and expanded the dockyards and citadels at Halifax and Bermuda. On the Pacific coast in the mid-1850s the Royal Navy made its base at Esquimalt, Vancouver Island, in support of British imperial interests. In the Atlantic and Pacific, British squadrons served to counter the rise of American land power. On the other side of the border, Americans took similar military precautions. Clearly, the "undefended border," as some historians in the twentieth century would call it, was mythical.[5] In Canada the prospects of an American military invasion loomed large. They remained so until the last boundary dispute, over Alaska, ended in 1903 and an Anglo-American accord had been reached.

The Empire of the St. Lawrence and the Fur Trade

After 1763, therefore, Canada had twice been invaded by Americans and twice defended by British arms. Though this would affect the perspective of British-Americans—a point to which we will later return—it must be noted that the British Empire was more than a military system. It was primarily a commercial system of metropolitan dominance and colonial subservience. Accordingly, in British America, colonial oligarchies and entrepreneurs were part of the larger system. And the political developments of the period 1763 to 1867 were tied in great measure to the shift under which the British Empire was going, from protection to free trade.

The commercial development of Canada after 1763 was largely based on staple production in furs, flour, and lumber. Donald Grant Creighton, in his great *Commercial Empire of the St. Lawrence, 1760–1850* which first appeared in 1937, wrote of how the St. Lawrence was the basis of the Canadian east–west political and commercial system. Canadian merchants especially from Montreal and Toronto, he argued, found inspiration in the St. Lawrence and its tributaries; they had commercial and political attitudes which were

5. See C. P. Stacey, "The Myth of the Unguarded Frontier, 1815–1871," *American Historical Review*, LVI, no. 1 (October 1950), 1–18; Kenneth Bourne, *Britain and the Balance of Power in North America, 1815–1908* (London: Longmans, Green and Co., Ltd., 1967); and Barry M. Gough, *The Royal Navy and the Northwest Coast of North America, 1810–1914: A Study of British Maritime Ascendancy* (Vancouver: University of British Columbia Press, 1971).

conditioned by the hard facts of geography and environment; they made attempts at exploiting the transcontinental river system leading to the St. Lawrence; and they made continental links with the northern interior of North America on the one hand and links across the North Atlantic with Britain and France on the other. This explained the non-American nature of Canadian development until the collapse of the Empire of the St. Lawrence in the 1850s with the introduction of canals and railways and the triumph of reciprocity with the United States in 1854.

In its environmentalist focus, Creighton's theory duplicated in some respects that of the historian of the American frontier movement, Frederick Jackson Turner. It gave weight and sophistication to Canadian historical development. But it failed to explain fully the development of the Canadian character, for not all Canadians were to come within the imperatives of the St. Lawrence River system and reflect its ambitions and outlook. Creighton, like Turner, has had his critics, but the development of the commercial system of the great river was central to Canadian history and an outline of this development does much to explain how Canada became a transcontinental nation.

With regard to the fur trade, the Conquest in 1760 brought a steady inflow of American and British entrepreneurs into Montreal, Trois Rivières, and Quebec. Even before the peace was signed in 1763, English, Scottish, and American fur-traders were reported "as thick as Muskettos" on the rivers flowing into James Bay. These "Pedlars from Quebec" continued to penetrate the waterways of the Canadian Northwest and Southwest and to extend the network of trading and supply posts developed by the French in the Indian lands, particularly of the Ojibwa and Cree. To the north of them, on sturdy posts built of wood and stone, sat their foe, the Company of Adventurers of England Trading into the Hudson's Bay, whose charter of 1670 allowed its members to be lords and proprietors in Rupert's Land—the land drained by waters flowing into Hudson's Bay—for the mere cost of paying the king two elks and two black beaver should he enter the territory—an unlikely possibility. These two rivals were separated by the dense coniferous forest on the edge of the Canadian Shield. This area was broken only by major river systems—the Churchill, Nelson, Severn, Attawapiskat, and Albany, to name a few—which provided trade arteries to and from the interior to the coast. The traders on the Bay were content to let the Indians come to them, and by sending gifts into the interior they exercised trading influence over an area radiating 1,500 miles inland from their posts. The "Pedlars from Quebec" countered this influence and that of the French on the Bay by penetrating into the high country itself. The Hudson's Bay Company responded by building posts inland, such as Henley House (1743) and the great Cumberland House (1774). The Canadians out of Montreal countered by pushing farther inland to the Churchill River, and in 1778 Peter Pond crossed into Athabaska—the new northern fur preserve of the Mackenzie River watershed—by way of the Methy Portage. This trade rivalry meant the extensive exploitation of the environment by Indians. Moose were exterminated in 1829 in this area, for instance. Thus European trade, from the Bay and from Montreal, had in its own way disrupted the ecological stability of the lands between Lakes Superior and Huron and Hudson and James bays. Moreover, tribal boundaries and Amerind social structures were changed, and by the early nineteenth century all Indians north of Lake Superior were in a dependancy relationship with the many trading posts on the bay and in the interior. This imperial process was to have other parallels elsewhere in Canada at other times.

This continental race for control of the North American fur trade pitted the Montrealers, using the methods, knowledge, and techniques of the French and Indians, against the English company operating out of "the Bay" and the Americans operating out of New York, Boston, and later St. Louis. On the north, the Montreal routes were up the Ottawa River through the Great Lakes to Lake Winnipeg, along the Saskatchewan system to the Peace River system, and then overland to the Fraser and Columbia watersheds. The routes from Hudson Bay were, first, from York Factory upriver to Winnipeg and thence into the Montreal routes and second, from Churchill to Lake Athabaska, Great Slave Lake, and the waterways of the Mackenzie, Peace, Fraser, and Columbia. A look at a map of Canada will show that the two routes, from Montreal and from Hudson Bay, were bound to collide in southern Manitoba.

The strategy of the competitors naturally centered around outtrading the rival. Montrealers attempted to intercept Indians on the way to the Hudson's Bay Company posts. The Indians were willing to accept a lower price for their furs because this saved them a lengthy trip to the Bay. As has been noted, this caused the companies to build new posts farther inland. But it had another result. The Montreal merchants had been competing among themselves for the Northwest trade. Most of them decided, in 1784, to pool their resources and agree to regulations controlling their trading practices. The result was the North West Company, and it included as partners Simon McLavish, Joseph Frobisher, James McGill, Peter Pond, Alexander Mackenzie, Simon Fraser, and David Thompson, many of whom were members of the prestigious Beaver Club of Montreal.

On the southern frontier, the Nor'westers sometimes cooperated with, sometimes competed with, American companies, especially those of John Jacob Astor. By 1813 they had purchased Astoria at the mouth of the Columbia from the Americans. They had established the first transcontinental commercial enterprise. Their fur empire stretched from Montreal some 3,000 miles westward to the Columbia River mouth. They had agents in London, Boston, New York, and Canton, and so vast were their operations in Canada (a trip from Montreal to the Northwest and back taking two years) that Fort William at the head of Lake Superior developed as the central meeting place of the trading (or winter) partners and the merchant (or summer) partners.

Lacking a charter similar to that of their British rival, the Nor'westers continued to lobby the British government for guarantees, but without reward. They were forced to rely on their own determination and energy; they had to win the contest against the English company or die. Not surprisingly, therefore, they sought new sources of furs. In the period from 1789 to 1813, Mackenzie, Fraser, and Thompson mapped the major waterways of northwestern North America and discovered new areas of exploitation and searched for possible trade routes to the Pacific. In 1789 Mackenzie located the river which now bears his name; and in 1793 he reached the Pacific overland from Canada, the first white man to cross the continent north of Mexico. In turn Fraser and Thompson explored the watersheds of the Cordillera and opened up the great continental fur trade of the northern Pacific slope. All three were responsible for building advance posts, some of which are now urban centers.

The Hudson's Bay Company, no less energetic, used different

methods to check its rival. In 1811, Thomas Douglas, fifth Earl of Selkirk, a Scottish philanthropist and idealist, acquired from the Hudson's Bay Company (in which he was a substantial stockholder) a grant to 116,000 square miles of land in what is now southern Manitoba, North Dakota, and Minnesota. Selkirk hoped to relieve distress of Scottish and Irish peasants at home and keep them in the British Empire by giving them arable land in Rupert's Land. These settlers, he argued, would provide food for the Company and thereby save it money. And positioned along the Nor'westers' thoroughfare to the Athabaska country, they were strategically situated to cut off the rival's trade and provoke the Métis who claimed the area as their own. By 1815 the conflict between companies had reached decisive proportions. In the following year in the Battle of Seven Oaks, near the forks of the Red and Assiniboine Rivers, the Nor'westers defeated Hudson's Bay Company forces and drove the settlers from Red River. Meanwhile, Selkirk, acting without legal right, decided to retaliate and seize Fort William. This proved to be a costly mistake. Various court cases went against him and he returned to Europe a broken man and died in France in 1820.

These developments hastened the union between the two companies. Rivalry had been shown to be fruitless. Only a merger could bring peace on the traplines and in the fur posts and also good relations with Indians and Métis. Moreover, only in this way could the Selkirk Colony be saved. The union, effected in 1821, has been aptly summarized by one historian as follows: "The final union of the rivals was at once a victory and a defeat for each. The Hudson's Bay Company was victorious in that its supply route by the bay triumphed over that by the St. Lawrence as did its charter over the partnership of the North West Company. It was defeated in that it won only when it adopted in large part the techniques and methods of its rivals inland. The North West Company lost its name and legal entity, but not before it had forced on its great competitor the mode of operation and the labor force which it had developed and by which it flourished. The united company was very much the old North West Company operating out of Hudson Bay." [6] The Company was

6. W. L. Morton, "The North West Company: Pedlars Extraordinary," *Minnesota History*, XL (Winter 1966), 164–65.

a unique amalgam of English capital, Scottish determination, Métis labor, and Indian purchasing power; and at its head was the dictatorial Sir George Simpson, who, one trader wrote, combined "the despotism of military rule with the strict surveillance and parsimony of the avaricious trader." In the vast domain of Rupert's Land and westward to the Pacific, the Company held sway, holding this quarter of the continent for the British Empire and establishing the unique, corporate character of the Canadian western frontier. The controlled relationship with the various Indian tribes, undisturbed by rivals except on the fringes of trade, allowed for a different, less violent form of white-Indian contact than in the American West.

The merger had important consequences because the Canadian fur trade, from Labrador to Vancouver Island and from Oregon and north to the Arctic, was now under the complete control of the Hudson's Bay Company. No board of directors in history has controlled a larger tract of real estate.

London was the metropolis of this frontier after 1821. Montreal declined as a center for the trade, and this was a development detrimental to the commercial interests of the empire of the St. Lawrence. The Hudson's Bay Company, having the ear of the British government and opposing American and Russian expansion on the frontiers of their trade, controlled a goodly portion of North America in the pre-settlement period. It was in many ways the vanguard of British and thus Canadian control in the Canadian West and far West. The geographical unity of Canada thus owes much to furs as a staple product in national economic development. But the Selkirk Settlement, which grew steadily and unnoticed by the outside world, was a portent. It showed by its existence that agriculture was possible on the plains. This was a fact in which Ontario businessmen, Quebec bishops, and British imperialists took an increasing interest as the nineteenth century progressed.

But Canada in the early nineteenth century was not a fur-trade colony alone. There were other economic occupations on the farms, in the forests, and on the seas. The abundance of natural resources and the structure of British mercantilism meant that the main occupation of businessmen in Halifax, Toronto, and Montreal was acting as middlemen between staple producers and British commercial houses. They did not develop a strong indigenous industrial system that would compete with Britain, "the workshop of the world." Instead, they concentrated their energies and capital on building a strong transportation system, first by sea and later by sea and rail, to relate sources of supply to overseas markets allowed for under British mercantile regulation.

This was the colonial economic context, and it meant that Canadian bankers, working in conjunction with local colonial oligarchies, identified with expanding transportation interests more so than with struggling industrialists. This mercantile oligarchy preferred to profit from trade and commerce rather than industrial production. Their cities, especially Montreal and Toronto, were rivals for dominance in trade—industry was of secondary importance. New banks, insurance, railway, canal and telegraph companies, and breweries emerged in colonial cities. New steamship services such as Samuel Cunard's in Halifax brought United Kingdom markets closer to British America, and a vast shipbuilding industry was built up in the Atlantic provinces, producing clipper ships, such as the *Marco Polo*, which were second to none on the Britain-to-Australia run.

We ought not to find it surprising that British North American capitalists felt betrayed when the British mercantile system, built up since the mid-seventeenth century on principles of interdependence, suddenly came to an end in the period 1846 to 1849 with the advent of free trade. Gone was the preference their staples enjoyed in British imperial markets. The solution, many Montreal merchant-traders believed, was to seek entry into the United States on fair and equitable terms. To this cadre empire was primarily a bread-and-butter proposition, and their Annexation Manifesto of 1849 was a reflex action of a colonial-oriented economy seeking a new metropolitan association. They repudiated ancient loyalties and then proceeded to destroy the commercial empire of the St. Lawrence by rejecting their old trans-Atlantic associations in an era of expanding world trade and, simultaneously, developing continental trade with the United States.

The Montrealers were not alone. In the Maritimes, as well, producers sought access for fish, lumber, and farm crops in the growing markets of eastern United States cities. They looked on railways as inducements to trade with the great cities on the St. Lawrence and in the American Midwest and Northeast. Prosperity in the golden age of wood, wind, and water was not to last forever. The transformation of maritime society was involuntarily underway by the mid-nineteenth century because the four colonies offered no new resources to markets that were undergoing an industrial revolution. They owed their existence to the sea, but the sea kept them divided one from the other. Local identities were strong, and they could not think in terms of a political reorganization that would provide a national ethos.

Momentarily, the Maritimes and the Canadas found a solution to their economic problems in the Reciprocity Treaty of 1854. This established free trade in the products of the sea, farm, and forest and granted the British North American colonies and the United States mutual use of the Atlantic fisheries and of coastal and inland waters. It was a continentalist scheme; and its legacy was that Canada became more North American in character, less tied to the imperial fabric that had given it birth.

All of these colonies were receiving emigrants from Great Britain in the nineteenth century. New lands were being thrown open to settlement; new industries were springing up, particularly in Ontario and Quebec. Settlers were pouring into Quebec, Montreal, and Halifax in great numbers. In the period 1815 to 1840, some 500,000 persons left from Great Britain and Ireland for British North America (418,000 went to the United States, 58,000 to Australia, and 10,000 to South Africa). Some of the early emigration schemes, such as Lord Selkirk's to Red River, were based on private philanthropy. Others, mainly government-sponsored, were based on the motives of improving the condition of the working class and at the same time providing a bulwark of loyal settlement on the southern Canadian frontier against American expansion. To British political economists who did not understand that certain government officials were seeking to increase the value of British colonies and not burden them with the dregs of British society, these schemes resembled a policy of "shovelling out paupers." In such places as Halifax, associations such as the Poor Man's Friend Society sought to help the poor and needy. Such organizations were not without their critics: in Halifax for instance, followers of Thomas Malthus, the English political economist, argued that the society encouraged the poor to be idle and irresponsible. Poverty and ungodliness went hand in hand. The critics often won the day, as in Halifax, and immigrants were forced to fend for themselves. Indeed, until the late nineteenth century when the social gospel had found widespread support, the "condition of Canada" question received little attention. But during much of the century, the position of the poor and indigent was not sufficiently described. More attention was probably given to prohibition and temperance—whose adherents related economic loss and crime to "liquid fire and distilled damnation"—than any other social ill. Economic productivity and godliness were the chief moral objects of Victorian society in Britain and the Empire, and all social problems were gauged by their contribution to those goals. Poverty and drink were evils which the Victorians, in their own ways at home or in the colonies, sought to eradicate.

This influence was not as dominant in Quebec as elsewhere. There the society was inward-looking: the parish took on more importance than it had during the French regime and its heart, either the village or the seigneurie, served as the center of professional services and labor. The new villages grew up around the church and its influence on the social mores of the community, especially family structures, was great. Because lands were not available in abundance to the *Canadiens* (the English controlling their disposition either through patronage or speculation), the villages and seigneuries became more densely populated. The *Canadiens* did leave the lowlands to settle townships on the margins of the Shield north and west of the St. Lawrence River in the early 1800s, where New Englanders, Scots, Ulstermen, and Irish Catholics were also to be found. The timber industry—providing squared timber for British shipbuilding industries—was the main livelihood and agriculture was carried on where soils were suitable. The *Canadiens* also settled in the Eastern Townships lying between the seigneuries and the American border. Loyalists had predated them and Irish, English, Scottish, and mainly New England settlers would follow after 1830. In the great towns of Quebec, Montreal, and Trois Rivières the *Canadiens* found themselves in increasing numbers after 1830 (a reversal of the trend in the period 1763 to 1830). Montreal, twice as large as Quebec in 1871, had 107,000 people, and its financial dominance over the lower St. Lawrence and its tributaries was well established. About 30 percent of Montreal's population was English-speaking. Upriver and on the north shore of Lake Ontario, Toronto was the main financial center of a hinterland inhabited in the 1860s by more than 1½ million people. Most were English-speaking—Pennsylvania, New York, and New

England land-seekers, Loyalists, Scottish crofters, Glasgow weavers, and Irish tenant farmers. There were others as well—Mennonites from Pennsylvania and Alsace-Lorraine, and Quakers. Large land tracts were granted them under proprietary, individual, or company auspices, and after clearing the forest they built log cabins, corduroy roads, and rudimentary bridges. Gradually towns emerged—invariably on river banks of the well-watered Ontario landscape. Mills for grains and timber sawing were centers of economic occupation in these urban clusters spread across the peninsula. Divided from the United States by Lakes Ontario, Erie, and Huron, though linked nonetheless by the Niagara peninsula and steamship services, Ontario society was provincial in perspective and proudly British and anti-American. War, the imperial relationship, and environment had shaped this view and as in Quebec the principal complaint of the populace was overpatronage and land control. Protestant denominations vied for church lands and influence in education.

By 1850 the population of southern Ontario was about one million and apart from Toronto it was a small town and a rural population. The opening of the Erie Canal in 1825 and the enlarging of the Lachine Canal at Montreal in 1848 allowed more seaborne commerce to reach Kingston, Toronto, and Hamilton, the result being that Montreal no longer remained the metropolitan center of the Canadian interior. Technological developments, especially the coming of railways and steamships, were bringing Ontario ports or inland cities directly into contact with Europe, the cities of the Atlantic seaboard, and the American Midwest. By the 1860s Toronto and its satellite urban centers were occupying a central position in British North American commerce. Free trade with the Americans in the period 1854 to 1866 provided additional stimulus for southern Ontario commerce. By Confederation, then, Ontario pioneers, favored by a central geographical position, British capital, and the influences of American economic growth, had laid the foundations of an empire of trade and influence beyond Ontario boundaries.

The British North American Revolution

The imperial relationship that channeled trade and capital, influenced values and mores, abolished slavery, and defined the European-Indian relationship through Crown or company influence also gave birth to a new type of political arrangement within the British Empire—a federation, the purpose of which would be to bring the British-American colonies voluntarily into an association conducive to trade, self-defense, and self-government. This system presupposed that the colonies would be self-governing—that is, be responsible for their own local affairs while remaining dependent on the Mother Country for defense, constitutional review, foreign policy, and the like.

The type of government existing in the British-American colonies after 1791 had proved increasingly unsatisfactory to the middle class, who believed oligarchic government was bad government. In the Canadas, strong vested interests operated from their seats of power in the colonial capitals of York and Montreal. In Lower Canada, the *Chateau Clique* of appointed English and French officials and parasites close to the governor wielded the predominant political power. In Upper Canada, to cite another case, the Family Compact of ultra-conservatives close to the governor controlled the colony's policy, contracts, development, and patronage. One historian has described this group as "a local oligarchy composed of men, some well-born, some ill-born, some brilliant, some stupid, whom the caprices of a small provincial society, with a code all its own, had pitchforked into power." [7] Nova Scotia, New Brunswick, Newfoundland, Cape Breton, and Prince Edward Island had similar oligarchies and similar problems.

These forms of government were unsuitable for the changing times of the 1830s and 1840s when industrialization, urbanization, and commercialization were providing new economic occupations for some and displacing others. In Lower Canada, the situation was critical, because *Canadiens* were facing an identity crisis perhaps as important as the Conquest that was proving to them that they were a nation besieged and inward-looking. Their nascent nationalism and class consciousness sought political liberties and economic advancement. In Upper Canada, the situation was no less critical, but there the question of race did not predominate. Rather it was a conflict of class, in which reformers sought to control the few who enjoyed the

7. W. Stewart Wallace, *The Family Compact: A Chronicle of the Rebellion in Upper Canada* (Toronto, Glasgow: Brook and Company, 1915), p. 7.

unchecked influence of Church and State. Throughout the 1820s and 1830s these contests for control intensified, and by 1837 the militants in both of the Canadas had become separated from the reformers. No less important, the vested interests strengthened their control, and subsequently remonstrances were signed, and rioting and rebellion broke out. The attempts by Louis Joseph Papineau, the eloquent Montreal lawyer, and William Lyon Mackenzie, the hotheaded Toronto newspaperman, to replace oligarchic government with more democratic models of American or French origin were crushed by force, and the rebellions came to an end. But the underlying causes of economic and political inequality remained.

Thus the rebellions never became revolutions: small armed resistances to the established colonial oligarchies occurred, not widespread desires for an overthrow of the system as expressed by Mackenzie's social democracy or Papineau's own brand of Jacksonian democracy. The majority of colonists in British America decried revolutionary procedures, as did the British government, whose authority in Canada was generally respected and desired.

Canadian society was never again the same. Some rebels, like Papineau and Mackenzie, fled to the United States. Others, not so fortunate, were sent to the public scaffold. About 119 political prisoners were transported to Tasmania and another 58 to New South Wales. Others were exiled to Bermuda. As for the two leaders, Papineau and Mackenzie, they returned to Canada in 1844 and 1849, respectively, under terms of amnesty. By the Amnesty Act of 1849 full security for all who had engaged in the rebellions was given by the Crown, and some returned from the Australian colonies or the United States. But Canadian society was taking on a new form. The influence of authority and the courts was in the ascendant. Caution became a byword for those who opposed the Establishment. The Yankee-born Marshall Spring Bidwell, a leading, quiet, and moderate critic of the Upper Canada government, bade goodbye to Canada, leaving its political society somewhat the worse for his exit. The laboring masses who had complained of injustices in 1836 and 1837 began an unending migration to the United States. In all these effusions, rebellion, its causes and its aftermath, left a stamp on Canadian society. Henceforth Canadians would point to the United States as a society rife with lawlessness and would pride themselves, somewhat mistakenly, with having purged their land of rebellion and violence forever.

Even so, the rebellions of 1837 served as a warning to the Colonial Office and Parliament that the links of empire were fragile, that another revolution in North America was possible. And although in the late 1830s and early 1840s the attitudes of British ministers toward the Canadian governmental problem stiffened, by the mid-1840s they favored reform. In 1838 the government of Lord Melbourne sent Lord Durham to British North America to investigate. He took with him a tremendous entourage, with plate, race horses, field marshall's uniforms, and two advisers—the well-known colonial reformers Edward Gibbon Wakefield and Charles Buller. This mission by "one of the most splendid swells of his time" reflected the British ministry's awareness of the need for an inquiry into the colonial problems of the British-Americans. His object was to find a formula to prevent the dismemberment of the Empire.

In his celebrated *Report on the Affairs of British North America,* presented to Parliament in 1839, Durham noted: "I expected to find a contest between a government and a people." He wrote of Lower Canada, "I found two nations warring in the bosom of a single state: I found a struggle, not of principles but of races; and I perceived that it would be idle to attempt any amelioration of laws or institutions until we could first succeed in terminating the deadly animosity that now separates the inhabitants of Lower Canada into the hostile divisions of French and English." And he reported of the *Canadiens:* "They are mild and kindly, frugal, industrious and honest, very sociable, cheerful and hospitable, and distinguished for a courtesy and real politeness, which pervades every class of society. The conquest has changed them but little. . . . It has left them without the institutions of local self-government that would have assimilated their character and habits, in the easiest and best way, to those of the Empire of which they became a part. They remain an old and stationary society in a new and progressive world."

In the following fashion he condemned French-Canadian society to a position of secondary importance: "I believe that tranquility can only be restored by subjecting the Province to the vigorous rule of an English majority; and that the only efficacious government would be that formed by a legislative union." In 1840 the British government passed just such legislation; and the Act of Union which created a new Province of the Canadas (Canada East, Canada West) commenced an unsuccessful experiment in biracial legislative conduct that would only be remedied by Confederation in 1867.

Yet Durham's main recommendation—responsible government—did not find a legislative base until 1846, when Sir John Harvey, the governor of Nova Scotia, was obliged to follow Colonial Office instructions that it was "neither possible nor desirable to carry on the government of any of the British provinces in North America in opposition to the wishes of the inhabitants." Henceforth, as responsible government spread through the white settlement colonies of the Victorian Empire, colonial governors and local autocrats were directly responsible to elected assemblies. Only in matters of foreign relations, external trade regulations, constitution-making, and disposal of public lands were Westminster's and the governor's hands visible. This also had been recommended by Durham.

In the Canadas also, the Governor-General, Lord Elgin, followed Colonial Office instructions allowing colonial ministers to exercise final responsibility in domestic issues. In 1849, the passing of the Rebellion Losses Bill, as a step toward a more democratic society in Quebec, came almost concurrently with the implementation of free trade principles. Gone were the days of mercantilism and imperial commercial advantage, and the consequent repeal of the English corn laws in 1846 brought cries of betrayal from the mainly English-speaking group who dominated the commercial world on the lower St. Lawrence River. Their Annexation Manifesto in 1849, mentioned previously, bewailed the apparent casting adrift of the colony on a stormy sea. Their remedy, they stated, consisted of "a friendly and peaceful separation from British connection and a union upon equitable terms with the great North American confederacy of sovereign states." But it was Elgin's negotiation of the Reciprocity Treaty with the United States in 1854 that silenced most of the critics, whose complaints rested almost solely on economic and commercial grounds.

This movement of the Canadian assemblies toward controlling local affairs has been classified by Canadian historians, in somewhat Whiggish terms, as "the winning of responsible government." They have seen the movement as one of progress. It is more accurate to say that the means of influence were more widely distributed after 1849 as the assemblies gained the political initiative. These historians have also claimed, but rightly this time, that the British North American experience was unique in Commonwealth history and that British colonies such as New South Wales, Cape Colony, and New Zealand were the beneficiaries of the reform movements in the Canadas. The governors Durham and Elgin, the rebels Papineau and Mackenzie, and the reformers Robert Baldwin, Sir Louis-Hippolyte LaFontaine, and Francis Hincks have become international figures in Commonwealth history. In short, the British North American revolution of colonial self-government within the British Empire therefore had important repercussions around the world.

Canadian Confederation

Yet in the mid-Victorian age self-government was insufficient in itself and the British-Americans had federation and nationhood almost thrust upon them by the circumstances of the times. In the 1860s the 3½ million colonists of British North America were faced with an issue that was central to their future: What chance did they have against almost ten times their number in the United States? Very little if they remained as separate entities; at least half a chance if they formed a union. The evolution of Canadian Confederation reflects the response to a challenge from within and outside British America.

It would be incorrect to say that the British public of the 1860s wished to be rid of Canada. More correctly, the British government sought a solution to its North American commitments. But politicians in power in Britain as well as in British North America considered undesirable a complete separation of Mother Country and colony: the monarchical connection was to be retained, and Britain's political and commercial interest in British North America was to be continued. Although "Little Englanders" such as Lord Brougham had many supporters in both houses of Parliament, the evidence is overwhelming that historians have all too often viewed the middle decades of the nineteenth century as being dominated by anti-imperial attitudes, and the result of this has been the rise of the myth of the "Little England" era. Yet few if any ministers of the British cabinet ever voiced opinions or wrote on the benefits of the separation of the

British North American colonies from the Mother Country. In fact, there is evidence that the British ministers sought, as they had in 1776 and 1812, to protect Canada from falling into American hands.[8] In the mid-1840s, for instance, Lord John Russell felt that a British North American federation would bring the colonials into the international community in a close alliance with Great Britain.

Confederation as we now know it was a design conceived mainly by colonial minds with the help of imperial pressures from Whitehall and with the aid of British officials in the colonies. It was primarily the colonial politicians who, with British support, solved the problems of the early 1860s and brought about a viable state out of colonies with widely divergent views.

Great historical developments have their celebrated causes and the achievement of British North America's Confederation is no exception. First of all, Confederation offered a solution to the bottleneck in the legislature of the United Province of Canada. Between May 21, 1862, and June 30, 1864, no less than five different ministries held office. Thus, Confederation for both Lower Canada and Upper Canada meant a solution to a deadlock in a legislature which after 1858 had been more or less plagued by the problems of equal representation of the two areas and of the political in-fighting associated with the system of double majority (where a minstry held power through a majority of influence among members from both areas). To George Brown, the leader of the Reform Party of Upper Canada and the initiator of the design for union, representation by population was the only solution to deadlock. To French-Canadians, "rep by pop" was a threat to their political influence. In the 1860s the problem of duality of culture was more important to the provinces now known as Ontario and Quebec than it was to the other colonies considering union. And it remains today primarily an issue between the two giants in the Canadian union, Ontario and Quebec, but has implications in the recent all-Canadian consciousness of and concern for or resentment about Quebec.

A second compelling factor was the American Civil War and associated with it the defense needs of British North America. The list

8. John S. Galbraith, "Myths of the 'Little England' Era," *American Historical Review*, LXVII (1961), 38–39.

is long of crises and events which strained the diplomatic relations and threatened war between Britain and the United States: the *Trent* affair, the *Alabama* claims, the *Chesapeake* affair, the St. Albans raid, Seward's passport scheme, the Fenian raids, and the projected abrogation of the reciprocity treaty with the United States along with the Rush-Bagot Convention forbidding either nation from maintaining armed cruisers on the Great Lakes. An equally important influence on British and Canadian opinion was the effect of the jingoistic cries of members of the American public, notably Secretary of State William Seward, who saw the territories north of the American border as an integral part of the United States. This was the challenge of Manifest Destiny. The English press prophetically contended that the present fear of invasion dictated a union of the British North American colonies. Even when the American Civil War had ended, many in the colonies asked themselves if the army of the victorious North—then the largest and most powerful standing army in the world—would turn on the relatively defenseless and long-sought-after British possessions to the north. And even when the crisis of American invasion appeared to have passed, in 1866, colonial legislatures from Nova Scotia to Vancouver Island, fearing Fenian invasions, took steps to protect the Crown in British North America from Irish republican sympathizers who believed, mistakenly, that any blow against the British Empire would aid the cause of Irish independence.

Thus a mutuality of defense needs necessitated a union of the British North American colonies; and with Confederation came the organization for bringing internal military security and a militia scheme. All this seems to point to the fact that the British provinces stood defenseless, without Britain's support. Yet this is far from the truth. In the War of the American Revolution, in the War of 1812, and in the war scare of 1845–1846 over the control of Oregon, Britain had proved that she intended to defend her colonies at all costs. Though in the 1860s Britain was anxious that the colonies should defend themselves, the Duke of Newcastle, the Colonial Secretary, stated in 1862 that the policy of British North America's defense was shared by the imperial as well as by the colonial governments. A union for defense was one need which all the colonies had in common, but the British connection still provided security.

The Canadians were also afraid that American expansionists, particularly from Minnesota, would gain the British Northwest—that vast, vacant territory lying westward beyond the settlements of Ontario where the Hudson's Bay Company maintained nominal British control. Between Lake Superior and the Rockies, Métis and Indian fur traders and buffalo hunters occupied a vast hinterland virtually unprotected by settlement except at Red River. Canadians understandably asked themselves how they could best safeguard this territory as the American frontier of agricultural settlement rolled steadily toward the British Northwest.

In 1857, the question of the renewal of the Hudson's Bay Company charter was debated in Britain and in British North America. The Company was, a free trade critic noted, "like a commercial tomb closed with the key of death to all except a favoured few." Such views bulked large in Parliament, where a committee of inquiry urged that there be no boundary between Hudson's Bay Company and Canadian lands. Their *Report* concluded that Canada's western boundary was the Pacific Ocean. They thereby recognized the future transcontinental nature of British North America. Active and influential British parliamentarians such as Robert Lowe, the Vice-President of the Board of Trade, and William Gladstone, the Chancellor of the Exchequer, destroyed the attempts of Sir George Simpson of the Hudson's Bay Company to prove that the interior of North America was a frigid waste unsuitable for agriculture and settlement.

Nonetheless, the British Parliament decided not to suspend the Hudson's Bay Company charter, and the principal reason behind this seems to be that by opening the frontier the balanced relations between the Company and the Indians might be destroyed. Canadian land-seekers, backed up by a growing Canadian awareness of their North American destiny of a Canadian nation from sea to sea, were incensed by the government's decision. Various newspapers, especially the Toronto *Globe*, edited by George Brown, a Father of Confederation, and *The North American*, edited by William McDougall, later lieutenant-governor of Manitoba, attacked the Company's trading monopoly in Rupert's Land. In 1857 members of the Toronto Chamber of Commerce petitioned the Canadian government to press for the end of the monopoly. The Speech from the Throne opening the 1858 session of the Province of Canada's legislature called for the annexation of the Northwest. But Brown was critical and in his *Globe* of April 19, 1859, he warned that if the coalition ministry of Macdonald and Cartier did not prosecute Canada's claims to the Northwest, "the prairie region of British America would remain sacred only to Indians, fur-growers and fur traders." Brown argued that the fur trade should be centered on the St. Lawrence and not on the Hudson Bay route to England, and in some ways it can be argued that the Federation of 1867 was the means of Canadian westward expansion, the political expedient for including the Canadian West within the empire of the St. Lawrence.

But the old imperial domination of the Company of Adventurers of England trading into Hudson's Bay would soon end and the days of settlement and of railways and of Canadian dominion would follow. When George Brown joined the Macdonald-Cartier ministry in June of 1864, his policy of Northwest annexation became government policy. In the minds of British and Canadian politicians, the British Northwest was to be protected for Canada, and in 1869, as we shall see, the paramountcy of factors and traders was at an end and with it a new chapter of occupation of the Canadian West begun.

It was in the final cause of Confederation—the need for an intercolonial railway—that the British played a most influential role in promoting union. The men of the City of London—the Baring Brothers, Watkin, Brydges, and others—made possible the capital for what was then one of the most ambitious of projects, an intercolonial railway that would link Halifax with the commercial empire of the St. Lawrence by 1,200 miles of track by way of Rivière du Loup. Wheat, fish, timber, and soldiers would be carried on rails totally on British-American soil and this would be done throughout the year, whereas formerly the frozen St. Lawrence River brought trade between the provinces to a stop in the winter months. For the Maritime provinces, a railway union was perhaps more important than any other Confederation influence. Indeed, the terms of union—the British North America Act—proclaimed that the construction of a railway was "essential to the consolidation of the Union of British North America, and to the assent thereto of Nova Scotia and New Brunswick. . . ."

The British North America Act of 1867, which defined the Dominion of Canada, signified the achievement of two interrelated British Empire precedents: decolonization and federation. As early as the

1830s early champions of Confederation had emerged. But in 1858, Minister of Finance A. T. Galt, put forth the first operative plan for a project of national magnitude. He suggested a federal union of all the provinces with local government in the Northwest. It was his farsighted financial design correlating the practical issues of railways and the public debt which the legislature of the Province of Canada adopted as the foundation of union. But when their delegation to London proposed that discussions take place on union, the Colonial Office maintained that federation was an issue dependent on imperial and not colonial initiative. Although the years that followed witnessed the growing importance of the Colonial Office as the Empire's executive authority, the initiative passed in 1860 to the colonies when the new Colonial Secretary, the Duke of Newcastle, dispatched a circular to the British North American colonies stating that the imperial government would consider any plan for union that the colonial legislatures proposed.[9]

Four years later, in 1864, representatives of the British North American provinces convened to discuss union at Charlottetown, Prince Edward Island. Originally the conference was called to discuss only a regional union of the Maritime provinces. But the Province of Canada sent a delegation captivated by a national idea: the union of all the British North American colonies. A second conference met at Quebec in 1865, where 33 representatives formed a constituent body and accepted 72 resolutions, which they ultimately presented to the imperial government as the suggested system of union. Brown, who presented the scheme of the Province of Canada, proposed a federal system of government with provisions for local governments in each province, and with provisions in the constitution for the eventual inclusion of the Northwest, the Pacific colonies, and Newfoundland in the grand scheme. The Maritime provinces agreed, providing the imperial government would guarantee the all-important intercolonial railway project. The grand design was taking shape and London newspapers such as the *Daily Telegraph* on November 25, 1864, reported that "no project of modern times rivals in boldness and vast-

9. W. L. Morton, *The Critical Years: The Union of British North America, 1857–1871* (Toronto: McClelland and Stewart, Ltd., 1964), pp. 78–79. See also, generally, P. B. Waite, *The Life and Times of Confederation, 1864–1867: Politics, Newspapers, and the Union of British North America* (Toronto: University of Toronto Press, 1962).

ness the proposed union of the British dominions on the American continent."

But the struggle did not terminate with the ending of the Quebec conference, for the provinces had to agree to the terms of union defined by the Quebec delegates. Politicians toured the provinces speaking on the subject of union, and the issue was hotly contested. In New Brunswick, the elections of 1865 resulted in a momentary reversal for the Confederation movement. However in the following year, Leonard Tilley and the pro-Confederationists were elected, ensuring New Brunswick's entry. In Nova Scotia, the anti-Confederation movement and the alienation of the influential newspaperman Joseph Howe posed a threat to the success of union. However, the ministry of Charles Tupper eventually brought Nova Scotia into the union. Even in 1868 Nova Scotians were dissatisfied, the House of Assembly voting unanimously for a repeal of the B.N.A. Act. The Colonial Office consequently took a firm hand, and convinced the Assembly that Nova Scotia's entry into Confederation was legal and binding.

Two other Maritime provinces rejected the terms of union as being detrimental to their interests. Prince Edward Island withdrew despite the facetious remark made by Thomas D'Arcy McGee, "the pen" of Canadian Confederation, in 1865: "Prince Edward Island will have to come in, for if she does not we will have to tow her into the St. Lawrence." As for Newfoundland, many there considered Confederation a dangerous Canadian project in which the economic advantages of being a British colony, and Britain's oldest colony at that, would terminate. The terms of union were not yet satisfactory or the times not yet sufficiently pressing for these eastern colonies to join the federation. With "continuous communication" guaranteed, Prince Edward Island joined in 1873. Newfoundland saw the advantages of union and entered Confederation in 1949.

There was little chance that the legislature of the Province of Canada would reject the Confederation terms that they had proposed at the Charlottetown and Quebec conferences. The Parliament of 1865 opened with these important words in the Speech from the Throne: "the circumstances of the times afford the opportunity not merely for the settlement of a question of Provincial politics but also for the simultaneous creation of a new Nationality. . . . With the public men of British North America it now rests to decide whether the vast tract of country which they inhabit shall be consolidated into a state, combining with its area all the elements of national greatness." [10] Each politician had ample opportunity to speak at length and it is from the *Confederation Debates* (1865) that the following points of view are drawn.

John A. Macdonald, Confederation's chief architect, explained that if British North America would have "one government and one parliament, legislating for the whole of these peoples, it would be the best, the cheapest, the most vigorous and strongest system of government we could adopt." But Macdonald explained that this was impracticable because in the first place "it would not meet the assent of the people of Lower Canada because they felt that in their peculiar position, being in a minority, in case of a junction with the other provinces, their institutions and their laws might be assailed." Like Quebec, the Maritime provinces did not wish to lose their identities in a legislative union.

A federal system was the alternative. "We have avoided the weak points of the United States Constitution," Macdonald noted; "we have avoided exciting local prejudices against the system of protecting local interests, and, at the same time, have raised a strong Central Government." For Sir E. P. Tache, who presided over the conference, the confederation design meant the preservation of Lower Canada's autonomy and the protection of "all the institutions it held so dear." But A. A. Dorion, a growing voice for French-Canadian interests and an advocate of strong local government in the union, was not convinced that the proposed form of Confederation was the answer for Quebec. "Everywhere this scheme has been protested against and appeal to the people demanded," he argued, "and yet in defiance of the expressed opinions of our constituents we are about to give them a constitution the effect of which will be to snatch from them the little influence which they still enjoy under the existing union. We are about on their behalf to surrender all the rights and privileges which are dearest to them, and that without consulting them." But Sir N. F. Belleau, a prominent Conservative, told the house that be-

10. Province of Canada, Assembly *Journals*, 1865 (1st session), p. 9, quoted in P. B. Waite, ed., *The Confederation Debates in the Province of Canada, 1865* (Toronto: McClelland and Stewart, Ltd., 1963), pp. ii–iii.

cause Quebec was to have 65 seats in the new union, this influence would enable her "to make and unmake governments at pleasure, when her interests shall be at stake or threatened."

The power of the Macdonald-Cartier-Brown coalition, however, was incontestable. Dorion's motion, as Leader of the Opposition, that the Canadian people, "fully appreciating the blessings of their political relations with the Great Empire of which they form a part, neither wish nor seek to create a new nationality" was soundly defeated by a vote of 64 to 25. When the Province of Canada came to vote on the Confederation issue the representatives from Lower Canada were not as agreeable to it as were those from Upper Canada. Only 37 of 62 members from Lower Canada voted for Confederation (of which only 27 of 48 French-Canadians concurred). But no less than 54 of the 62 members from Upper Canada supported Confederation. The union was thus a concept which did not have the unanimous support of the Province of Canada in the 1860s. More than a century of Confederation experience has shown that the fears expressed during the 1865 Confederation debates in the Province of Canada were justified.

The 72 resolutions passed during the Quebec Conference and accepted by the provinces which joined the federation formed the basis of a constitution. With Colonial Office assistance this document was worded in the form of a bill for the consideration of the Imperial Parliament. In 1866, at the Westminster Palace Hotel Conference, representatives from the Province of Canada, New Brunswick, and Nova Scotia discussed the Confederation terms with officials of the Colonial Office. In the following year, Parliament considered the legislation in only four short sessions in the Commons and only one meeting in the Lords. One observer in the Commons remarked that the members gave only "pronounced indifference" to the British North America bill. In the Lords, the Colonial Secretary, the Earl of Carnarvon, championed the passing of the bill. After giving full praise to the Canadians for their initiative, determination, and careful planning to effect a union, Carnarvon urged that the House agree without change to "the treaty of union" of the "consenting parties." The British North America Act of 1867 received royal assent on March 28, and on July 1, 1867, the union of the British North American provinces under the name Dominion of Canada came into being.

Canadian Confederation was designed to create what Lord Monck, the Governor-General, referred to at the Dominion's first parliamentary session, in November 1867, as "the foundation of a new nationality." The new nation-state was not to be unilingual or uniracial. Rather it was to bridge the gap between races and to link isolated communities of differing ethnic backgrounds under the Crown. From the beginning, then, the Dominion of Canada was predicated on a calculated risk as to whether or not this "new nationality" of the architects of Confederation could be erected and made safe for years to come. Having no community of race, language, and religion, and living in close proximity to the United States, French- and English-speaking Canadians of 1867 had to possess a state of mind of great optimism.

Their Confederation idea fired the imagination of many men. From Vancouver Island to Newfoundland, citizens, politicians, businessmen, and newspaper editors contributed to the debate. It was, we are told, "literally a national issue, the first and the greatest that British North Americans had to face." [11] Some British North Americans were bent in 1867 on overcoming the geographical and ethnic obstacles that faced them. They were obsessed with the dream of nationality and somewhat frustrated by the yoke of colonial status. They saw in Confederation the opportunity of transcending their narrow colonial identities, of breaching Canadian political deadlock, and of creating a transcontinental state. They aspired for a "new nationality" within the British Empire and a chance to take their place in the world. In 1867, George Etienne Cartier, a Father of Confederation, could boast: "Henceforth we shall rank among the nations." He and his associates must have known the difficulties in forging a new nation-state into being, where centrifugal forces of diversity and race pulled counter to the tendencies toward union.

11. Waite, *Life and Times of Confederation,* p. 4.

4

Dominion Expansion, 1867–1896

Four colonies constituted the new union of 1867 within the British Empire and under the monarchy. The federation allowed for a strong central government which would deal with national matters, but at the same time the constitution was to give expression to local interests in the provinces. Further, it was a scheme for transcontinental dominion. Yet the Canadian Confederation of 1867 was not an end but a beginning, and the subsequent quarter century of dominion expansion would reveal great divisive issues that threatened the national strength at the center and correspondingly aided the local interests in the provinces. This process has not stopped, except during the two world wars, when centralizing tendencies were strong. In our own times, the tensions of federal-provincial relations are an extension of earlier problems between the national capital in Ottawa and the various capitals in the provinces.

The legislative instrument of the new Canadian state was the British North America Act. Effective July 1, 1867, this British parliamentary statute announced in its preamble that the provinces of Canada, Nova Scotia, and New Brunswick desired to be federally united into one Dominion under the British Crown with the constitution "similar in principle" to that of the United Kingdom. Such a union would contribute to "the Welfare of the Provinces and promote the Interests of the British Empire."

The most significant feature of the new federal structure was its powers at the center—as enumerated in Section 91 for "peace, order, and good government." John A. Macdonald, the chief architect of union, never tired of stressing that Parliament and the central government were to have a commanding position in the new system. He and other Fathers of Confederation sought to avoid the weaknesses and mistakes of the United States' federal system by giving residual powers to the federal government in addition to giving it all the major subjects of legislation. He would have preferred a legislative union but his counterpart from Canada East, Cartier, insisted on a federal scheme, for he believed, we now know foolishly, that it would protect the cultural identity of the French through the role of the upper house or Senate. The Senate, the weaker house, differed from its American counterpart: members were appointed by the federal government on the basis of equal representation for the regions rather than the provinces. Powers of appointing lieutenant-governors and supreme court judges and disallowing provincial legislation were vested in the federal government.

The use of English and French languages was guaranteed by the British North America Act. These languages could be used in Parliament and the courts of Canada, and in the legislature and courts of Quebec. Education and its regulation by Church or State was a burning issue in the nineteenth century. Section 93 of the Act allowed provincial legislatures exclusive control of education but elaborate safeguards on the rights of denominational or separate schools operated to protect minority interests, denominational affiliations, and sectarian interests. Section 93 was thus not a "blank cheque" for the Catholic church in Quebec, or, as events were to show, for the Protestants in Manitoba or Ontario. In sum, French-Canadian cultural features of language, education, and civil law were accorded recognition in places where they existed in 1867. But whether or not the Fathers of Confederation proposed to extend their application to other parts of the nation where French-Canadians might eventually live would be a subject of continuing interest and controversy where minority interests seemed threatened.

The Canada of 1867 consisted of only four provinces—Quebec,

Ontario, New Brunswick, and Nova Scotia were the only participants in the bold experiment. In the East, the colonies of Newfoundland and Prince Edward Island rejected the terms of union. The promise of an intercolonial railway from Halifax to Montreal and Toronto and the prospect of their legislatures being debt-free were insufficient attractions to offset the fears of being out-voted by the larger numbers of central Canada. Canadian tariffs, also, were no viable alternate for these colonies on the periphery of a state centered on the St. Lawrence. The coming of Confederation coincided with the end of the age of wind, wood, and water; as Stephen Leacock later wrote, "the shades of night were falling and the night was called Confederation." [1] Even in Nova Scotia and New Brunswick, colonists had second thoughts on the "Botheration Scheme." In the former, Joseph Howe led an abortive attempt at secession in 1867. In the latter, New Brunswick toyed with a similar plan for separation in 1868 but this came quickly to an end during the Fenian scare of that year.

In the West, the Confederation project was also unresolved. Rupert's Land, a Hudson's Bay Company chartered territory since 1670, was in effect promised Canadian land after a British parliamentary report of 1857 recommended ultimate union. But the terms of transfer had yet to be worked out and the few thousand residents of the Red River settlements lay within easy reach of Minnesota expansionists. In the far West, the United Colony of British Columbia lay at a great length from the Empire of the St. Lawrence and was situated precariously between Washington Territory and the newly acquired American possession of Alaska. Largely unsettled but possessing substantial gold and other mineral reserves, its vulnerability to invasion by American "marauders without title," Russian gunboats, or angry Fenians from San Francisco was mollified by the salutary presence of ships of the Royal Navy's Pacific station with a base at Esquimalt from mid-century onward. And the political loyalties of the colony were by no means settled in 1867; for economic reasons, annexation to the United States might provide a better alternative to a union with Canada.

Thus the Canadian Parliament that met in November 1867 faced formidable barriers to the projected transcontinental state.

1. Quoted in Frank H. Underhill, *The Image of Confederation*. The Massey Lectures, 1963 (Toronto: Canadian Broadcasting Corporation, 1964), p. 6.

Nova Scotia and Joseph Howe had to be pacified; and the shrewd Macdonald granted a larger federal subsidy to the province and brought Howe into the cabinet as minister in charge of provincial affairs. But he held firm with the imperial government against any constitutional changes to the British North America Act which would have allowed Nova Scotia to withdraw. By January 1869 Nova Scotia had been secured for the union.

Manitoba and the Canadian West

The next task for the Canadian nation-builders was acquiring Rupert's Land, that vast territory which lay north and west of the Canadian Shield and stretched westward to the Continental Divide and northward to Arctic shores and beyond.

At the time of Confederation, British politicians were prepared to end their territorial obligations in North America. Canada's ownership of Rupert's Land would give greater solidarity to the British North American provinces at a time when American Manifest Destiny doctrine threatened to engulf the whole of North America. In London, therefore, the Colonial Office looked with favor on the rounding out of Canada to attain natural transcontinental limits. As mentioned earlier, in 1857 the House of Commons enquiry into the affairs of the Hudson's Bay Company had recommended that Canada should take over the Red River and Saskatchewan areas, and should do so as soon as possible, because Minnesota had a bulging population in relation to Rupert's Land. In fact, Minnesota was to attain statehood in the following year, 1858, and the steady progress of the American frontier of settlement and business was closely watched in Toronto by persons such as George Brown, editor of *The Globe,* and by William McDougall, editor of *The North American.* At the same time, *The Northwester,* a Fort Garry newspaper, agitated for union and communication with the St. Lawrence. We have already seen how uncertain the early Selkirk Settlement at Red River was in its early days. By the 1860s some 2,000 Europeans formed the only sizable settlement of its kind in the West, and the Canadian government looked with paternalistic eyes on its possibilities. The early history of Manitoba in becoming a province in Confederation was to be played on a larger scale of international and continental rivalries, and this was a contest in which Canadians such as Macdonald, Cartier,

Brown, Galt, and McDougall were shown to be expansionists imbued with their own brand of Manifest Destiny.

Canadian and American rivalry for the Red River area increased after July 1866, when the United States House of Representatives considered, but did not pass, a bill for the admission of all the British North American colonies, the Selkirk Settlement, Saskatchewan, and British Columbia into the Union. Macdonald and his cabinet colleagues aimed to forestall any such American design. Acting without assurances being given that local interests would be respected, in 1867 they asked the imperial Parliament to transfer the rights of the Northwest from the Hudson's Bay Company to Canada. Perhaps no one thought of asking the Métis. Had an effort been made to consult local authorities and the government of Assiniboia they might have averted the resistance of 1869–1870 and, in some respects, the 1885 rebellion in Saskatchewan. By a simple real estate transaction, the Rupert's Land of 1868, the Crown got back the land title from the company and bequeathed it to Canada. For this, surely one of the largest transfers of territorial sovereignty in history, the company received £300,000 and one-twentieth of the western lands. A company that had sought immunity from settlement now sought profits from land sales in the "fertile belt," and the "frozen wastes" of the West that Sir George Simpson so artfully described to the parliamentary inquiry of 1857 were soon to become a place for Canadian civilization, administered by Ottawa.

The Canadian government set October 1, 1869 as the date of transfer and sent McDougall west by way of St. Paul to be the first lieutenant-governor. He was accompanied by his aide-de-camp, Colonel J. S. Denis, who brought with him fifty rifles with which to arm a new body of militia. McDougall, an arch Canadian expansionist, lacked diplomatic skills. When he approached the 49th parallel north of the settlement of Pembina he expected to get a welcome from the queen's new subjects. Instead, he got the following letter from the force of Métis or mixed bloods: "The National Committee of Métis of Red River informs Mr. McDougall that by order he is not to enter the territory of the Northwest without special permission of this committee." This letter, dated October 21, 1869, was signed by John Bruce, president of the Métis council, and Louis Riel, the secretary. No English Métis or Canadians had flocked to McDougall's support; instead, his position had no popular basis, and his proclamations in Victoria's name fell on deaf ears.

The Métis had little desire to allow Canadian expansion into an area where they had their own primitive society and economy based on the dwindling buffalo herds, the fur trade, the freighting of goods on their squeaky Red River carts and *bateaux* between Forty Garry and St. Paul, and farming in the old *canadien* manner with strips of land running to the banks of the Red or Assiniboine Rivers. Their origins date from the earliest contact of French fur-traders with the Huron and Algonkin women of the mid-seventeenth century, and by 1869 this society with rich strains of Indian, French, and Scottish blood numbered about 10,000 in Red River alone. They were formidable hunters who excelled at guerilla warfare. These colorful, multilingual and bicultural persons formed a society in which immorality, roistering, and drunkenness were sure to sadden the travelling priest. "Unwashed and barbarous and infested as it was," Stegner has written in *Wolf Willow*, "this was the germ of a culture that could have come to something in its own special terms if history had been kind." [2] But history was not kind.

The leader of this volatile and energetic society was Louis Riel, perhaps the most enigmatic figure in Canadian history. Considered by some to be a rebel, by others a patriot, he made a profound influence, only recently understood, on Canadian political history.[3] Born in St. Boniface, Assiniboia, in 1844 of Métis parents, he developed an early interest in leading this "New Nation," as he called it. Serious, introverted, and radical, he was found at the Collége de Montréal to be unfit for the Roman Catholic priesthood. Nor was he suited for a career in law. By 1868 he was back in Red River and assumed the leadership of the Métis. It was he, not Bruce, who led the resistance against McDougall.

Riel's next move was to seize Fort Garry with the help of 100 followers on November 2. This daring act, executed without opposition, gave the Métis control of the major cache of supplies and munitions in the colony. Here he was advised by clerics, comrades, and certain American expansionists whom Macdonald derisively called "Yankee wire-pullers." An independent "New Nation" might have

2. Wallace Stegner, *Wolf Willow* (New York: Viking Press, 1962), p. 65.

3. Because Riel's achievement was "not a positive one" he was not included among the twenty-five "great Canadians" selected by Vincent Massey and others in 1965. See *Great Canadians: A Century of Achievement* (Toronto: The Canadian Centennial Publishing Company, 1965). Subsequently, biographical studies have appeared, Manitoba has granted him belated recognition, and he has been the subject of a number of plays and an opera.

been Riel's ultimate objective, but one wonders if some sort of annexation to the United States was not high on his list of alternatives.

In Ottawa, meanwhile, Macdonald and the cabinet knew that they would have to pacify the Métis in order that the Canadian grand design of westward expansion would not be obstructed. Macdonald wanted to negotiate with the Red River Settlement as a whole, not with Riel alone. He hoped for a quick deal with Riel's provisional government by which he could thereby forestall American expansion. Consequently, he sent Donald A. Smith, head of the Hudson's Bay Company in Canada, to arrange a settlement, distribute £500 in gifts, and appease the Métis. Already well-respected at Red River, Smith forced Riel to call a general meeting of the inhabitants, and from this came a list of Métis demands. Macdonald was prepared to allow the "list of rights"—which included provincial status, separate schools, and protection of minority rights. In short, he was ready to yield in the face of Métis pressure, and became increasingly aware of the French-Canadian influence on the federal government for the development of a French-speaking and Catholic dominion in the West which would counteract the growing Anglo-Saxon preponderance of Ontario.

This seemingly beneficial movement toward accord was interrupted by the execution of Thomas Scott. An Ontario Orangeman living in Red River, Scott actively opposed the provisional government and supported the Canadian party's abortive rising in February. Moreover, he held the Métis in contempt. Jailed for assault, he was found guilty, perhaps justifiably so, of "insubordination and striking the guards." Riel would hear nothing of Smith's appeals for mercy. "We must make Canada respect us," Riel told Smith, and so, on March 4, 1870, a rifle squad killed Scott in the snows outside of Fort Garry. Overnight, Scott became a symbol for English Canada and a martyr of Ontario; and his cause was taken up by the Liberal party. Macdonald, however, was not to be deflected from his planned course of action. He established, by Act of Parliament of May 1, 1870, a new province called Manitoba, meaning "the God that Speaks," with representation in the Senate and House of Commons. Local government, separate schools, and minority protection were all guaranteed, and the protest in Red River diminished. It was small in size —only 11,000 square miles, of which 1,400,000 acres were reserved for the Métis.

Riel stayed at Red River until August. When Colonel Garnet Wolseley, quartermaster-general in Canada, and two battalions of troops who had paddled and marched from Canada, approached the deserted Fort Garry, Riel was nowhere to be found. He had, in fact, left for the United States. Riel was not content to remain outside Canada, however. In 1873 and 1874 he was elected to the House of Commons, but on both occasions he was not allowed to take his seat. In 1875 he obtained amnesty on grounds that he would remain in exile for five years. This was certainly a curious form of justice, but it took the heat off Prime Minister Alexander Mackenzie, whose followers would have preferred to have had Riel tried or perhaps lynched for the "murder" of Scott. From 1875 to 1884 Riel remained, for all intents and purposes, out of Canada. He was in several asylums during this time and also taught in the Jesuit mission of St. Peter's not far from Great Falls, Montana. Here, on June 4, 1885, four horsemen brought Riel an urgent invitation to lead a second resistance against the Canadian government.

We may wonder what Riel's first reaction to the invitation must have been. To have declined it would have been tantamount to negating his previous role as a leader. He knew well that the Métis, both in and out of Red River, had grievances on the question of land control. He knew that thousands had left Red River for the valley of the Saskatchewan, where they had founded settlements at Batoche, St. Louis, and St. Laurent. He knew that the building of the new Canadian Pacific Railway threatened the end of the buffalo hunt and the old agrarian order in the Northwest. And he knew of the "great awakening" among the tribes of western North America, and of the desperate conditions of the Indians in the Saskatchewan area. A food shortage in that region in the years 1878 to 1880 meant that the Northwest Mounted Police must feed some 7,000 people a day, and by 1884 the situation had become acute. Finally, Riel believed he was their chosen leader. Assuming the name of "David Mordecai," in keeping with his biblical and religious beliefs that the fall of Rome was at hand and that in himself a new leader had been proclaimed, Riel accompanied the four horsemen to the Saskatchewan area, where in the summer of 1884 he began a campaign for the redress of Métis grievances.

Riel arrived at the banks of the North Saskatchewan River in July 1884, just at the time the Indian agitation had come to a head.

First he met with the Stoney chief Big Bear and urged the Indians to form a council. Then, with T. J. Jackson, he drew up a manifesto and united the Métis for resistance against the Canadian authorities. On March 19, 1885, he proclaimed a provisional government at Batoche, the main Métis headquarters in the district. He was less successful in uniting the various Indian tribes and bands; the great Blackfoot Confederacy and the Crees—except for the bands of Big Bear and Poundmaker—remained uncommitted. Similarly, white settlers and English mixed-bloods remained aloof. The insurrection, then, was chiefly the work of the Métis and discontented Indians.

Riel's role in the preparation of the resistance was important, but it was based strongly on the earlier work of Gabriel Dumont, a tough, courageous, and able military leader. It was Dumont, not his hero Riel, who, as adjutant-general in charge of military operations, "harrassed Commissioner Irvine and his Mounted Police and General Middleton and his militia, beat the Mounties at Duck Lake, forced the abandonment of Fort Charlton, whipped Middleton's column at Fish Creek, disabled the steamer *Northcote* that was coming downriver to the aid of the militia besieging Batoche, and finally, against heavy odds and the overwhelming firepower of repeating rifles, 7-pounders, and one of the new Gatling guns graciously donated on a test basis by the United States, was driven out of Batoche and into hiding in the Birch Hills." [4] After the rising, Dumont found safety in Montana, worked in Buffalo Bill's Wild West Show, and toured Europe as a marksman, shooting glass balls out of the air. After amnesty was declared, he eventually returned to his beloved North Saskatchewan, where he died a peaceful death and was buried at Batoche in 1906, perhaps the last remaining symbol of the old militant Métis cause.

By contrast, the end was quick for Riel. He surrendered on May 15, 1885 in a state of despair and mental illness. He would soon face trial. Poundmaker and his followers surrendered on May 26. Their arrival at the Canadian military headquarters at Battleford was "the most pathetic and picturesque procession I have even seen," as one observer wrote. On July 2, Big Bear gave himself up and this brought the resistance to an end. At a cost of some $5 million, the Métis insurrection had been put down, and 5,000 troops and 400 horses had been put into the field and transported some 2,000 miles west by the

4. Stegner, *Wolf Willow*, p. 62.

Canadian Pacific Railway, which was not yet complete in every section but which was nonetheless proving to be of strategic value to Ottawa.

Such an overwhelming defeat for the Métis had longstanding consequences for them. As a cultural group they all but disappeared. Some found their way into the security of Indian reservations. Others moved north and west to escape the pressures of another civilization. They are still to be found in wretched settlements in northern Alberta, the Mackenzie River area, and on the banks of Great Slave and Great Bear Lakes. The Indians fared better: a general amnesty was proclaimed in 1886; the rebel Indians were punished but not vindictively; and the loyal bands were given generous concessions by the government. In 1896 the Canadian government negotiated a peaceful return of those Indians who had fled to Montana during the resistance. But they were wards of Ottawa nonetheless and the advancing Canadian civilization afforded them no mercy.

There were other results of the Northwest Rebellion that affected the politics and race relations of the country. The trial of Riel, begun on July 6, 1885, in Regina, the capital of the Northwest, became a national incident. Faced with the charge of treason, Riel was at once the patriot of French Canada and the rebel of English Canada. It is said that the ghost of the Canadian Ulsterman, Thomas Scott, stalked the courtroom and that the six jurists, all Anglo-Saxon and Protestant, were intent on obtaining revenge for the death of Scott in 1870. In Ottawa, Macdonald was intent that there should be a speedy resolution of the matter: Riel would hang, he wrote to a friend, "though every dog in Quebec bark in his favour."

After Riel made an incoherent speech in his own defense, the jury deliberated for a brief time and reported that he was guilty. Appeals from Canada and the world over could not save him. Nor could the politics of Canada. He was hung on November 16, 1885 and buried in the cathedral yard at his native St. Boniface. He had come, in many respects, full circle. But as a prophet he had failed to preserve a way of life that was dear to him, a way of life doomed to extinction. With him died the dream of a vast, autonomous Métis nation-state in the Canadian Northwest. The territorial integrity of Canada had been preserved but at a high cost to minority and ethnic interests and to the racial harmony of the nation, a fact not soon to be forgotten.

British Columbia

The creation of the new province of Manitoba in 1870 had been precipitated by resistance to Canadian authority. In some respects it had been forced into existence. British Columbia, by contrast, entered Confederation in a fashion that would provide the pattern for subsequent entries.

At the time of the new province's entry in 1871, British Columbia was the most isolated part of the British Empire. Its sole links with Canada were by seldom-travelled mountain trails; its links with the outer world were by long sea-lanes. In every respect, then, the colony was frustrated by the disadvantages of distance. Not surprisingly, relations with nearby American ports on Puget Sound and San Francisco were significant for the commercial and cultural development of the colony. In these circumstances, the colony's society was to reflect a close attachment to the Mother Country and, at the same time, exhibit a frontier spirit which only a land of extensive wealth in furs, gold, coal, and timber could produce. Decidedly Anglo-Saxon in temperament, white British Columbians were obsessed with their security vis-à-vis the neighboring United States, difficult coastal Indian tribes such as the Cowichan, Haida, and Tsimshian, and, in the late nineteenth century and afterward, the rise to world power of Russia and Japan.

The colonial history of the new province was rather brief in comparison with other settled areas of Canada such as Ontario and Quebec. The discovery of sea otters at Nootka Sound by Captain James Cook in 1778 had attracted the attention of fur-trading interests in various parts of the world. Within several years, various English firms and other Europeans had entered into the trade with Canton. The North West Company was active in exploring the territory overland, and in 1793 Alexander Mackenzie reached the Pacific after crossing the Rocky Mountains in the first overland crossing of the continent north of Mexico. He was followed by Simon Fraser and David Thompson, fellow Nor'westers, who began trading and exploring west of the Continental Divide in the mountainous region stretching from the Columbia River basin north to the Peace River region.

In addition to the interest of British and Canadian traders in the region, several foreign powers sent expeditions for exploration and trade. Spain in particular was anxious to retain her privileges in the eastern seas as defined in the Treaty of Tordesillas, 1494, and pressed her claim against British "interlopers" until the threat of war forced her to accept British claims to territory and trade at Nootka in 1790. The Russian American Company pressed south from Russian America or Alaska, and in 1824 and 1825 Russia made treaties with the United States and Great Britain defining the southern limits of Russian America as 54°40″ North latitude. The United States was similarly interested in the area and would not agree with Britain on establishing an Anglo-American boundary along the Columbia River. The Convention of 1818 between the two powers allowed for a no-man's land between 42° and 54°40″ North latitude. War was a near matter in 1846 but a resolution of this question came in that year. By the terms of the Oregon Boundary Treaty, the 49th degree of North latitude west of the Rocky Mountains and exclusive of Vancouver Island, which the British insisted should remain in their hands, established the western portion of the border.

The Oregon dispute underscored the conflict between fur trade and settlement in the Pacific Northwest. The Hudson's Bay Company, the dominant British force in the region after assuming North West Company trade there in 1821, could out-trade its American rivals, as it did in the Snake River country in 1824. Yet it could not hold on forever against the steady inrush of American settlers making their way overland on the Oregon trail. The British could not defend against the "Oregon fever" through British settlement, which would have been an anathema to a fur-trading concern. They could not protect the area by sending gunboats or troops. The retreat of the Company from its headquarters at Fort Vancouver on the Columbia was, in any case, concurrent with its shift of commercial interests. Coast trade could not be easily conducted from the dangerous Columbia, and in 1843 James Douglas (later Sir James Douglas, Governor of Vancouver Island and British Columbia), established Fort Victoria on the southern tip of the island; by 1849 this had become the focal point of Company operations in the North Pacific and on the adjacent North American mainland.

Reading the lesson of the Oregon crisis, the British government decided that systematic agricultural colonization would consolidate the area within the British Empire and preserve it against American squatter settlement. The government believed also that a British naval base at Vancouver Island would counter the American port of San Francisco and the rise of American naval power in the Pacific. In 1849, the Hudson's Bay Company, against many complaints of other commercial interests and individuals alike, received the rights of colonization to the island. The terms of such were designed to ensure that the Company would develop the land, not for the prolongation of the fur trade but for the development of British settlement in this remote quarter. The colony of Vancouver Island was to be a bulwark against American penetration at no cost to the British taxpayer. The birth of the colony was thus a product of the "preemptive impulse" which so characterized British imperial expansion in the mid-nineteenth century.

From its beginnings, the colony was foiled by its remoteness and the circumstances of the times. For one thing, the set price of land was £1 per acre, whereas in the adjacent American territories it could be purchased for a dollar or less. Accordingly, immigration was small. A second reason was that the Company and its agricultural subsidiary, the Puget's Sound Agricultural Company, acquired the best lands in and around Fort Victoria and Esquimalt, leaving the rocky hinterland and outlying areas to independent settlers. By 1852 no more than 450 settlers were on the island, and most of these were Company servants. Another reason for the slow progress of the colony was that the California gold rush drained off labor and put Vancouver Island at an economic disadvantage. In sum, the progress of the colony did not meet the expectations of the British government, and thus its future lay in doubt.

This condition was changed by the discovery of gold on the Fraser River and its tributaries in 1857. The rush that began in April 1858 was one of the greatest in history, and it attracted the dregs of society. Especially noteworthy was the arrival of Americans from the California gold fields, and British law and order on this turbulent frontier were maintained through the timely support provided Governor Douglas by British gunboats and the Royal Engineers. A system of justice was implemented under the "hanging judge" Matthew Begbie. These developments allowed for the peaceful evolution of the new colony of British Columbia, created by Act of Parliament in August 1858, in a fashion which was not generally typical of the North American frontier experience.

During the gold rush Douglas kept a firm hand on local affairs. The populace was too motley, too untrustworthy to be granted an assembly such as that granted to Vancouver Island in 1856, and so the governor ruled with or without, as the case might be, the help of a small council. The Fraser River rush ended almost as quickly as it had begun, and miners soon left for California and other areas.

In 1862 many of the same sort of persons were attracted to Williams Creek in the Cariboo country, where large gold nuggets were uncovered. This gave birth to the great Cariboo gold rush, and it attracted many Canadians, Europeans, British subjects, and Americans, some of whom were Southerners during the Civil War. Large, prosperous communities developed. Barkerville became the largest city in North America west of Chicago and north of San Francisco. The government built roads to these settlements and the Cariboo Road carried the wagons of the Wells Fargo and Barnard express companies. They were the scene for the passage of camels used unsuccessfully in that dry country. By 1865 the population in the gold fields declined as mining became more of a corporate operation. Now the government had on its hands an expensive road system, and the Cariboo Road had become a public liability. By this time also, Douglas had retired as governor of the Vancouver Island and British Columbia.

Douglas' successor in British Columbia, Frederick Seymour, had urged the maritime union of the colonies on the Pacific seaboard. "I should like to see the strengthening of British authority, British influence, and British power on the Pacific, and I at once admit that the existing division weakens all three," he advised the Colonial Office in 1866. In that year the two colonies became the United Colony of British Columbia, with the capital at Victoria. Rivalry between "the island" and "the mainland" was intense. The colonial debt was about $1,300,000, most of which had been run up by the mainland.

The prospects for a healthy colony were slim indeed, and the colonists began to take increasing interest in the necessity of responsible government and with it the possibility of union with British North America. A few persons urged annexation to the United States. In September 1866, a public meeting had declared for annexation, the beginning of a movement which was to lead to 43 of Victoria's 3,000 citizens signing an annexation petition in 1869. But the annexationists were more than countered by the Canadian faction, especially by Amor de Cosmos, the editor of *The British Colonist.* The Confederation movement was delayed for a variety of reasons, including the fact that the Northwest Territory had yet to be transferred from Hudson's Bay Company to Canadian control and also by the fact that Governor Seymour proved obdurate.

But in March 1870 the colonial executive and legislature had decided on union with Canada if the right terms could be agreed upon, and a delegation went to Ottawa to negotiate. The two parties agreed that the new province would have responsible government with provincial status. Her debt would be assumed by the federal government and the province would receive annual per capita grants and subsidies. British Columbia would also keep the British naval station at Esquimalt if Canada could persuade the Mother Country to maintain it and would be provided with a guaranteed loan for a drydock at Esquimalt. Most importantly, the new province was promised a railway link with Canada to be built within ten years. On these generous terms, British Columbia entered Confederation on July 20, 1871.

The government of Canada had struck a bargain with British Columbia. Macdonald, Cartier, and Galt had known that American expansion in Pacific America, especially since the Alaska purchase in 1867, made British Columbia's position insecure. As Galt put it, "If the United States desire to outflank us on the West, we must . . . lay our hands on British Columbia and the Pacific Ocean. This country cannot be surrounded by the United States—we are gone if we allow it. . . . We must have our back to the North." Now the Canadian dream of transcontinental dominion had been achieved by the addition of British Columbia. There was little love for Canada expressed by British Columbians, however. The relationship was to be judged on its economic merits. "The only bond of union outside of force," wrote the respected and pessimistic Dr. Helmcken of Victoria, "will be the material advantage of the country and the pecuniary benefit of the inhabitants. Love for Canada has to be acquired by the prosperity of the country, and from our children." No doubt these feelings are still apparent in British Columbia, where regional identities are particularly strong and the benefits of the national tariff are not immediately felt.

PRINCE EDWARD ISLAND

John A. Macdonald had achieved part of his dream by the extension of Canadian sovereignty over the Northwest territories and by the inclusion of British Columbia within the union. But he had not been entirely successful on the Atlantic frontier. Nova Scotia and New Brunswick had entered Confederation almost under protest, and in 1869 further negotiations with Newfoundland had been fruitless. After British Columbia's entry, Macdonald turned his attention to Prince Edward Island, which he knew would drive a hard bargain after the generous terms for British Columbia. Macdonald wanted full control over British North American fisheries in order to give the Canadian government greater leverage in dealing with the United States. And he wanted Prince Edward Island for another reason: it was a convenient smuggling base which lay beyond the Canadian tariff wall and was "so situated, and so blessed with harbours for small vessels, as to make it a customs-inspector's nightmare." [5]

For Macdonald, the negotiations with the Prince Edward Islanders were nearly as difficult as with the British Columbians. But here at least there was no possibility of annexation to the United States: geographical considerations forbade that. Every question was financial, and the Islanders knew full well that union with Canada would come eventually, and on terms very much to their liking.

The inhabitants of the Island had enjoyed little contact with the mainland since the colony's separation from Nova Scotia in 1769. The first half of the nineteenth century had witnessed the occupation of most available agricultural lands; and by 1871 some 94,000 settlers lived on the island, eating a regular diet of potatoes, oatmeal, salt cod, and pickled herring. Their economy was based heavily on lumber but by 1867 the forests had been cut and displaced loggers turned to agriculture. Here, however, they were faced with the limitations of the absentee landholding system. "The great bulk of the island," Lord Durham reported to the Colonial Office in 1838, "is still possessed by absentees, who hold it as a sort of reversionary in-

5. Andrew Hill Clark, *Three Centuries and the Island: A Historical Geography of Settlement and Agriculture in Prince Edward Island, Canada* (Toronto: University of Toronto Press, 1959), p. 120.

terest, which required no present attention, but may become valuable some day or other through the growing wants of the inhabitants. But in the meantime, the inhabitants of the island are subjected to the greatest inconvenience, nay, to the most serious injury, from the state of property in land. The absentee proprietors neither improve the land, nor will let others improve it. They retain the land, and keep it in a state of wilderness."

Thirty years later the land problem remained unresolved. Islanders saw in Confederation an opportunity of ending this handicap; they demanded $800,000 to be used for buying out the absentee proprietors. The Canadians considered this the next thing to extortion, if not the very thing itself, and so there was no union. Another reason for the collapse of the Confederation movement at this stage was that Prince Edward Islanders feared that they would not get adequate representation in Ottawa. The promise of only five members of Parliament, as given at the Quebec Conference in 1865, affirmed their suspicions that a small province such as theirs would surely be swamped and overlooked in the larger union. Even pressure from the Colonial Office in 1866 could not change their opinion.

After 1867 the Island tried to buy out the absentee proprietors. However, it became increasingly clear that only outside financial help could rid the colony of its burden. By this time, also, the colony—for reasons of local politics and pride more than necessity—had undertaken the building of an extravagant railway far beyond its means. The railway had been a losing proposition since its construction, and its existence convinced the colonists, who could not even make the interest payments, of the wisdom of making the Canadian government assume the colonial debt.

The terms of Prince Edward Island's entry into Confederation were made hastily in 1873. Canada granted the island a generous per capita annual subsidy of $50, provided $800,000 to buy out the absentee landlords, and guaranteed the railway debt and also continuous communication with the mainland.[6] The bargain was struck and in 1873 Prince Edward Island became the seventh province of

6. Since 1873 there have been several proposals for a tunnel (a "metallic subway" was the term used by Lord Granville, the Colonial Secretary, in 1886) to link the island with the mainland across Northumberland Strait. In 1929 the government estimated the cost at $40 million and the project was dropped. More recently there has been talk of a causeway.

Canada, a development which augured well, so the optimistic Macdonald thought, for shortly bringing stubborn Newfoundland into the new federation and thus completing the union of the whole of the Queen's North American possessions.

RAILROAD TO THE PACIFIC

The Fathers of Confederation knew well the values of a railroad to the Pacific. They understood that a railroad was more than an economic necessity; it was a political need, a material tie of empire, a transcontinental linking of the Atlantic seaboard, St. Lawrence waterways, prairie settlements, and Pacific ports. Though by 1876 the Intercolonial Railway linked Halifax with Montreal, a railroad west to the Pacific would complete the continental sphere of things for the nascent Canadian nation, forestall American northward expansion, and make, as one British Columbian put it, "a real live confederation with Canada instead of a paper one." The Canadian Pacific Railway was thus a catalyst; it gave the new Canadian provinces a common sense of purpose, a feeling of nationhood. But it remained to be seen whether or not a 3,000-mile railway could be constructed within the time or finances allotted to build this national dream.

The major question was how to finance this grand design. It could be a private venture, a government project, or a marriage of the two. The last of these, paralleling the experience in the United States and linking corporate expertise and capital with government assistance, was followed. Macdonald and his cabinet found capitalists willing to form a company, and in 1872 the charter was granted to Sir Hugh Allen, a Montreal shipping magnate and investor.

Allen, the public soon learned, had already contributed $300,000 to Conservative party coffers and the personal bankrolls of Macdonald and Cartier. The nation shook with amazement when it learned the damning evidence. A telegram from Macdonald to Allen, marked "immediate, private," and which read, "I must have another ten thousand; will be the last time of calling; do not fail me; answer today" broke the government. Macdonald was forced to resign in November 1873. In a subsequent election, in 1874, the Liberals and their leader Alexander Mackenzie, a former stonemason from Sarnia, Ontario, were swept into power. Macdonald and the Conservatives were to be in opposition for a four-year period. The "Pacific Scandal" of 1873 had brought discredit to the party and its leadership, a handicap not long to plague the Conservatives. Construction delays, inept Liberal attempts to pacify British Columbia ("the spoilt child of Confederation," according to the press), changes in route, and the great depression of the late 1870s went against the speedy completion of the railway.

By 1878 the Conservatives, now back in power, began a program to finish the road. Under the Canadian Pacific Railway Act of 1880 the national enterprise was given a new life. The corporation, dominated by George Stephen (later Lord Mountstephen) of the Bank of Montreal, Donald Smith (later Lord Strathcona) of the Hudson's Bay Company, and James Hill, a successful railway builder, received the government's blessing, a cash subsidy of $25 million, a land grant of 25 million acres "fit for settlement," and 700 miles of existing track. They were protected from paying taxes on their property and facilities for twenty years and were allowed twenty years (until 1900) to complete the project.

That this was the biggest corporate arrangement in Canadian history during the nineteenth century seems indisputable; that the government's support was generous seems undeniable. Yet the corporation was soon begging for more money and although Macdonald's earliest impulse was to reject any request, he well understood an adviser's warning that "the day the Canadian Pacific busts, the Conservative party busts the day after." An additional $27 million from the public purse was required to complete the railway. On November 7, 1885, the last spike was driven at Craigellachie, near Golden, in the heart of British Columbia's mountain wilderness.

Thus was the great project completed. The nation could no longer be called a "geographical expression." And although the railway would not bring immediate prosperity to the land through trade and settlement, it opened a new chapter in the history of Canada and its West, and would be important in the character of its evolution as noted below. At the same time, the railway spelled the demise of the plains society which Riel, Dumont, Big Bear, and Poundmaker had sought to preserve. In 1885, as we have seen, the Northwest Rebellion was put down by Canadian troops brought west on the new tracks. It also provided a new link in British imperial communications with Hong Kong and Australasia. The new cities of Sudbury, Brandon, Regina, Calgary, Revelstoke, and Vancouver were all born of the roadbed. In all these respects, Canada was an achievement of the railway age, and the railway became the symbol of the country.

Canada First and the National Policy

In 1874, at Aurora, Ontario, Edward Blake, a man soon to lead the Liberal party, spoke of the national objectives. "We are engaged in a very difficult task," he said, "the task of welding together seven Provinces which have been accustomed to regard themselves as isolated from each other, which are full of petty jealousies, their Provincial questions, their local interests. How are we to accomplish our work? How are we to effect a real union between these Provinces?"

Blake knew well that an interprovincial union had been arranged through Confederation; he also knew that the Canadian Pacific Railway would provide material substance to the new nation. But he had no easy solution as to how a national feeling, consciousness, or identity could emerge from this disparate, straggling Canada. Liberals and Conservatives alike promoted a Canadian patriotism; and the press, Parliament, and the public platform discussed the subject. But what unity could exist in such a ramshackle and diverse country where rational and ethnic identities and colonial sentiments took precedence over national feelings?

In 1868, shortly after Macdonald, Cartier, and others began erecting a constitutional framework for the new state and seeking the foundations of a "new nationality," five young men met in Ottawa to discuss the question of national unity. They were William A. Foster, a Toronto barrister, Henry J. Morgan, Charles Mair of Lanark, Ontario, Robert J. Haliburton of Halifax, a son of the author of "Sam Slick," and Colonel George T. Denison, later a president of the British Empire League in Canada. All in their late twenties or early thirties, these men formed the "Canada First" party. Denison, in his *Struggle for Imperial Unity*, later wrote of their meeting as follows:

> Nothing could show more clearly the hold that confederation had taken of the imagination of young Canadians than the fact that, night after night, five young men should give up their time and their thoughts to discussing the higher interests of their country, and it ended in our making a solemn pledge to each other that we would do all we could to advance the interests of our native land; that we would put our country first, before all personal, or political, or party considerations; that we

would change our party affiliations as often as the true interest of Canada required it. . . . It was apparent that until there should grow, not only a feeling of unity, but also a national pride and devotion to Canada as a Dominion, no real progress could be made towards building up a strong and powerful community. . . . History had taught us that every nation that had become great, and had exercised an important influence upon the world, had invariably been noted for a strong patriotic spirit, and we believed in the sentiment of putting the country above all other considerations—the same feeling that existed in Rome

When none was for a party
When all were for the State

This idea we were to preach in season and out of season whenever opportunity afforded.[7]

The Canada Firsters were among Canada's first nationalists and they believed that confederation was a creation without a soul, without a spirit that animated the nation, without a national identity. This near third party thought of the Conservatives and Liberals as men dominated by sectarian, political, and partisan interests, not national aspirations. Intending to be a nonpartisan group, Canada First was actually "Ontario First." They promoted the idea of securing for the Dominion British Columbia and Rupert's Land. With regard to the latter, its members supported Ontario interests in the 1869–1870 Manitoba resistance; they saw in Cartier and the Catholic church an alliance to protect Riel and French interests in the western settlements.

Soon they began publishing a new monthly magazine, *The Canadian Monthly and National Review*, and in 1874 a weekly, *The Nation*. New members or associates were attracted, among them the Liberal, Edward Blake. In 1874 they announced the founding of the Canadian National Association and the National Club. These groups were designed to promote the interests of "Canada first before party."

The proposals of the young Canada Firsters included keeping the British connection, consolidating the British Empire, and obtaining for Canadians a voice in treaties affecting Canada. They wanted closer

7. George T. Denison, *The Struggle for Imperial Unity: Recollections & Experiences* (London: Macmillan, 1909), pp. 10–12.

trade relations with the British West Indies, with the ultimate aim of political connection, an often repeated theme in the late nineteenth century.[8] They also wanted electoral, ballot, and legislative reforms along Chartist and later Fabian lines. Minority representation, immigration, militia reform, and more economic management of public affairs were also preached. Finally, and here they were most successful, they sought the imposition of a tariff, a duty applied to certain imports that would make them so expensive as to encourage Canadian industry.

But for all its enthusiasm, the Canada First movement began to disappear almost as rapidly as it had appeared. Edward Blake did not wholly support the cause. The group lost its momentum. Still, the nationalism that was expressed by Canadians in the late nineteenth century owed something to the Canada Firsters. It was John A. Macdonald's "national policy" of the protective tariff, the railway to the Pacific, and the settlement of the Canadian west which gave birth to the first long-lasting sentiments of Canadian nationalism.

Macdonald's national policy was not only a domestic policy of railway building, immigration settlement, and protective tariffs. It reflected a Canadian will to maintain a separate identity in North America. This was revealed in such matters as the North Atlantic fisheries dispute, the Bering Sea affair, Canadian-American trade relations, and the Alaska boundary dispute. However, it made its initial appearance in a time of economic difficulty. It is a well-known fact that Canada's economy is closely related to that of the United States. This was especially true in the depression of 1874–1879 in Canada, which paralleled that of 1873–1878 south of the border. As a staple trading economy, Canada was hit hard. The Liberals' remedy was to push for a new reciprocity treaty with the United States similar to that which had been in effect from 1854 to 1866. The Conservative policy was to construct a tariff.

The National Policy of 1878 aimed at national pride. Strengthened by their election victory of that year, Macdonald and the Con-

8. In this period, Canada, like other nations, was seeking a place in the sun, both in the Pacific and Caribbean. These ambitions, small as they were, have been considered in Merze Tate, "Canada's Interest in the Trade and Sovereignty of Hawaii," *Canadian Historical Review*, XLIV, No. 1 (March 1963), 20–42, and Robin W. Winks, *Canadian-West Indian Union: A Forty-Year Minuet* (London: Athlone Press, 1968). In 1974 these ambitions would again be noticed in respect to the Grand Turk and Caicos Islands.

servatives implemented high duties on various commodities, especially textiles and iron manufactures. The application of import duties came just as the depression was lifting. Exports increased dramatically; prices were buoyant; national revenues rose; immigration improved. Businessmen, farmers, and laborers benefited. Canadians consequently associated the high tariff with prosperity, much as the British North Americans of the 1850s and 1860s had associated reciprocity with prosperity. And the Conservatives got their reward in 1882 when they were reelected with as big a majority as that of 1878. "The good times was the only thing against us," bemoaned one Liberal to another.

The tariff was but one portion of Macdonald's three-cornered scheme of economic nationalism. More all-Canadian railways would be built to complete the union (as if the projected Pacific railway was not already enough) and encouragement would be given by the federal government to large-scale immigration and the settlement of the Canadian West. But the protective tariff remained central to the whole design: it would shape a national market, aid eastern industry and national transport, and help the agricultural interests of the nation. It formed, in spite of all its infirmities and the perennial controversy associated with it, the basis of nation-building for Canada. It constituted Macdonald's greatest achievement after 1867. Its influence is still felt in the present Canadian tariff structure.

Central to the national policy was the occupation and development of the Northwest Territories. Canadians saw in the broad prairie reaches a homeland for the sons of Canadian farmers and the energetic and hardy citizens of northern Europe, especially the United Kingdom. The Canadian West would do many things for Canada: it would counter American westward expansion, aid eastern industry, provide a northwest passage by land to British Columbia and the Pacific, and offer new national resources. Accordingly, the federal government maintained a tight control in the Northwest. It negotiated Indian treaties. It sent out the North West Mounted Police in 1874. It established a survey of the area in 1869. It allotted homesteads of 160 acres under the generous terms of the Dominion Lands Act of 1872. Finally, it allowed for a nominated council under terms of the Northwest Territories Act of 1875. As is discussed below, by 1905 these vast reaches had matured into the new provinces of Saskatchewan and Alberta, and the hand of the federal government was everywhere in their making. But in this development, the hardships and toil of the prairie settlers were no less important.

In its manifestations of railway building, immigration, settlement of the west, and the protective tariff, the national policy gave the country new substance. In 1879, Minister of Finance Sir Leonard Tilley had said, "the time has arrived when we are to decide whether we will be simply hewers of wood and drawers of water" or will "make this a great and prosperous country, as we all desire and hope it will be." For all its faults, the national policy did much to support the design of the Confederation Fathers. More particularly, the noncommercial object of founding and fostering a nation in North America separate from the United States was implicit in the national policy.

In these years after the American Civil War, Canada's position in relation to the United States was dictated by the hard facts of relations between Great Britain and the United States. In the period from 1861 to 1902, it is fair to say, the transatlantic rift of the two powers was eventually bridged. From a state of near war, the two English-speaking powers moved into diplomatic alignment, and this *rapprochement* was necessitated by the rise of the German Empire and the inability of Britain to maintain a balance of power in North America. Canada was caught in the demise of the *Pax Britannica.* Although up until recently it has been customary to see the development of Canadian autonomy as an inevitable and even beneficial movement away from the Mother Country's apron strings, a more plausible case can be made that the hard realities of British foreign policy in an age of *realpolitik* did much to determine the evolving, and at times uncertain, adventures of the new nation into continental and world affairs.

The Treaty of Washington, signed in 1871, brought understanding between the United States and the British Empire over certain issues. Some Canadian interests were set aside, partly because the British were looking for accord, partly because the Americans discounted the value of the British properties. By the terms of the treaty, each nation had access to the other's in-shore Atlantic fishing grounds for ten years, a development that did not favor the Canadians. Canada secured free access of her sea fish and fish oil to American markets. Her claims to compensation for losses in the fisheries were to be put to arbitration. So, too, was the San Juan Boundary question, a dispute originating in the poor definition of the boundary separating

Vancouver Island from the mainland according to the Oregon Boundary Treaty. Canada obtained no unrestricted commercial reciprocity with the United States. Nor did she get any satisfaction for her Fenian claims. The United States pressed hard its *Alabama* claims, and although Americans wanted Britain to exchange Canada for damage done to Union shipping by Confederate raiders such as the *Alabama*, put to sea under British surveillance, in the end the arbitration commission awarded the United States $15 million. In 1872, San Juan Island became American territory by award of the German emperor, Kaiser Wilhelm I. In 1877, the large award of $5½ million went against the United States for damage to the Canadian fisheries. In 1885 the United States abrogated the fisheries clauses of the Treaty, and this led to distress in the Maritime fisheries. All in all, however, the Treaty served to mollify issues of discord. It did much to strengthen the peaceful relationship of Canada and her American neighbor.

In terms of Canada's relationship with Great Britain, the Treaty had important implications. Macdonald, a member of the British delegation to Washington, had insisted that the Canadian Parliament ratify the Treaty, and this was done in 1872. Moreover, he believed it time for Canada to establish what he called "a healthy and cordial alliance" with the United Kingdom, a sort of free association denied the American a century before. In an era when Gladstone's government was withdrawing the imperial garrisons from all quarters of the globe, and those from Halifax and Quebec in 1870 and 1871, respectively, and was suggesting that Canada should consider some sort of naval defense, Macdonald was in no mood to equate the costs of defense with imperial solidarity. He told the House of Commons on May 3, 1872, when he was appealing for the ratification of the Treaty, that the severing of Canada from England was possible but not probable. He hoped, he said, to see Canada one day an "auxiliary to the Empire, and not a cause of anxiety and a source of danger."

But Canada, Macdonald knew, was not yet ready for independence. At least Canada had achieved its first role in treaty-making, and Canadians would later point to this fact with pride. Nonetheless, a purely Canadian delegation had been denied by the British Foreign Office because imperial solidarity in international treaty making had to be observed. And the terms of the Treaty did not meet Canadian aspirations. Problems of navigation, fisheries, and trade would frequently appear in Canadian-American relations, and for Canada it was an uneasy arrangement. The Alaska boundary dispute, with an outcome far less satisfactory to Canadians than that of the Treaty of Washington, would force the nation to take the initiative in dealing unilaterally with the United States in matters of international dispute.

Canada, we may note, was coming of age. The analogy of the poor child being neglected by her imperious mother *Britannia* and being sought in custody by her rich continentalist Uncle Sam is not wholly without validity. Yet it must not be forgotten that in an age of rising Anglo-Saxonism, Canada identified herself with the British Empire and gained national and world status thereby. No matter how strong the pulls of continentalism, the Anglo-Canadian alliance remained the essential foundation of the young nation's external policies.

Political Parties and Political Problems

The period 1867 to 1896, with the exception of the Liberal ascendancy of 1874 to 1878, belonged to the Conservative Party. It was a period dominated, as we have seen, by one of the most capable of prime ministers the nation would ever know, Sir John A. Macdonald. Well known as a Father of Confederation, Macdonald was the architect of Canadian transcontinental dominion, and the promoter of the Canadian nation to a position of associate status within the British Empire. A curious-looking man with a nose that had ripened with age and whisky, he had the ability to get to the heart of a matter. He never forgot that popularity was the basis of power. Nor did he ever forget that a cabinet of loyal and sympathetic colleagues would stand him in good stead.

Macdonald chose his associates wisely. His French-Canadian lieutenants were George Etienne Cartier and later Hector Langevin, both of whom commanded the support of the Quebec hierarchy. Macdonald held the Maritimes and the West by patronage and promises of railways, drydocks, and tunnels. His control in Ontario was less certain but his national policy appealed to business and labor, Orangemen and Catholics. Above all, Macdonald built a party that combined political cohesiveness and national policies.

By contrast, the Liberals offered the voters very little either in personnel or party. Only after the Pacific Scandal of 1873 did they enjoy power, and then only briefly. They were not to taste victory again until 1896. They stood for reciprocity with the United States, reform, temperance, and thrift. But they lacked clear alternatives to the monopoly of Macdonald and the Conservatives.

Only in provincial affairs did the Liberals make an impact before 1896. Sectional discontent, which was born in colonial times and not resolved by Confederation, was strong in Canada during the 1880s and 1890s. Much of it was inspired by the great depression of the late 1870s, which reduced Canadian productivity and induced Canadians to migrate to the United States by the hundreds. In Quebec, the Liberal premier, Honoré Mercier, a champion of *canadien* nationalism, complained of the abuses of federal disallowance of provincial legislation. Manitoba, anxious for more trade with the United States, wanted a repeal of the Canadian Pacific's monopoly of western rail traffic. Ontario, suffering from dwindling commerce, wanted "better terms," an increased federal subsidy. Nova Scotia and New Brunswick agitated for federal indemnification for the 1885 U.S. abrogation of fisheries clauses in the Treaty of Washington. The Maritime provinces, in general, were suffering from economic transformation in industry and transportation as old trades and markets disappeared, and Saint John and Halifax grew at the expense of smaller outposts. Maritime coal enjoyed protection in Canada but Ontario and Quebec manufacturers were regarded as exploiters.[9] Only British Columbia and Prince Edward Island remained content with Dominion-provincial financial arrangements.

Mercier's answer to sectional discontent was to hold an interprovincial conference in Quebec City in 1887. British Columbia and Prince Edward Island did not attend; the rest found agreement among themselves impossible. No concerted action could be agreed

9. *The Halifax Morning Chronicle* bitterly put it this way in 1886: "The people of Nova Scotia know the Ontario or Quebec man but we know him principally in the shape of the commercial traveller. He comes here to sell, but he buys nothing but his hotel fare and in this respect he makes a rather ostentatious display. He is usually a genial sort of person, has a diamond ring, smokes fair cigars, sets them up with the boys in an offhand way, and generally conveys the impression that in his own estimation he is a very superior being, whose condescending patronage it is a great privilege to enjoy. He spreads himself periodically throughout this province, in number he equals the locust and his visit has about the same effect. He saps our resources, sucks our money and leaves a lot of shoddy behind him. He has been able—at least the people whose agent he is—to have laws passed that compel us to buy his wares or submit to a tremendous fine if we purchase from John Bull or brother Jonathan." For an important historical perspective on the dynamics of projecting of Nova Scotia discontent on the "Upper Canadians," see George A. Rawlyk, "Nova Scotia Regional Protest, 1867–1967," *Queen's Quarterly*, LXXV (Spring 1968), 105–23.

upon, and the conference served little more than to give the provinces an opportunity to vent their feelings. Their attack on the Dominion government had failed; but for the first time they had opposed it en masse. This clearly meant that the fabric of a carefully contrived and centralized nation-state might give way to a less certain structure founded on particular provincial or regional interests.

Macdonald now found himself on the defensive and he gave in to the provinces on several things. He repealed the monopoly clause of the Canadian Pacific Railway Act. He rearranged tariffs to soothe the Maritimes. Above all, he gave up free powers of disallowance. Subsequently, all appeals in matters of dispute between federal and provincial governments under terms of the British North America Act were to be reviewed by the Judicial Committee of the Privy Council at Westminster. Until 1949, when the Supreme Court of Canada became the final authority, the Judicial Committee invariably sided with the provinces. That body held to the *letter* rather than the *spirit* of the British North America Act; and a dejected Macdonald was forced into recognizing that the residuary clause placed provincial governments not in a subordinate position to the federal government, as he would have wished, but in a position of equality.

At the heart of provincial discontent lay uncertainties about Canada's economic future. From 1871 to 1891 the population of the country stood at a standstill. The nation has been described as "a huge demographic railway station." In those twenty years, more persons left the country—mostly for the United States—than entered it as settlers. A slight increase in population occurred, but this was due to natural growth. By 1891, only 4,833,000 persons inhabited the sprawling reaches of the country.

In that same year, Goldwin Smith, formerly Regius Professor of History at Oxford University and a resident of Toronto after 1871, set down his potent analysis of the nation's problems. His *Canada and the Canadian Question* told of the inevitability of continental union. He wrote how each region of the country was tied inseparably to its American neighbor; how the English-French cultural impasse was insoluble; how Canada First was futile; and how imperial federation had little chance of success. His gloomy prediction caused many Canadians to ponder their future. Some, including Principal George M. Grant of Queen's University, looked on the book with disfavor. Grant argued that Canada could overcome the geographical and economic forces that Smith thought so binding. For Grant and his kind, Canada's "concept of power" lay in contributing to the British Empire.[10] Here then was the sharp difference between continentalism on the one hand and Anglo-Canadian accord on the other. It was a dispute that was to last well into the twentieth century.

In addition to the debate on the future of the country, two other issues arose in the late nineteenth century which revealed the nation's racial problems. The first of these, the Guibord affair, was more local than the second, the Manitoba schools question. Both, however, were concerned with the questions of civil rights and the interplay of Church and State.

The Guibord affair was confined to Quebec. There, a conflict developed between the *Rouges* or Liberals, who were anticlerical, agnostic, or merely felt religion should be divorced from politics, and the Roman Catholic Church, which was nationalist, conservative, and desirous of preserving the old order of close alliance between Church and State. The *Rouge* party and its *Institut Canadien* sought to oppose Macdonald and his Conservative dominance. Their blatant criticism of religious orders, illiberality, and Ultramontanism—all prevalent in Quebec—and their support of nonsectarian education was bound to meet with resistance. In 1869, Bishop Ignace Bourget of Montreal had the *Institut* banned on the grounds that it contained dangerous volumes in its library and it harbored perverse doctrines. In the following year the Vatican Council, by declaring papal infallibility, strengthened the Ultramontane cause.

Shortly after the 1869 decree, Joseph Guibord, a member of the *Institut*, died. He had been a devout Catholic, yet the clergy would not sanction his burial in a Roman Catholic cemetery and he was buried in a Protestant graveyard. The *Institut*, at death's door itself, pressed for the right of a citizen to be buried in the consecrated ground of his own church and took the case from court to court. Finally, the Judicial Committee of the Privy Council brought down a judgment favorable to the *Institut*. The Church, the Ultramontane press, and some of the Montreal populace protested adamantly. "No bloody xxxx will pass this gate! God damn Guibord!" was the feeling of one Catholic. Pressure from the Governor-General, Lord Dufferin, was brought to bear and on November 16, 1875, six years after his death, Guibord was buried in the Côte des Neiges cemetery in Mon-

10. George Munro Grant, *Canada and the Canadian Question: A Review* (Toronto, 1891); and Carl Berger, *The Sense of Power: Studies in the Ideas of Canadian Imperialism, 1867–1914* (Toronto: University of Toronto Press, 1970).

treal beside the body of his wife. The Church, however, could not be denied its sacerdotal functions: the Bishop deconsecrated Guibord's grave, thus giving the Church a hollow victory over which the State could have no dominion. But in its larger consequences, the Guibord affair was a triumph for civil rights in Quebec. Although the *Rouges* and the *Institut* had dug their own grave and the Quebec by-elections of 1876 brought gains for the Conservative or *bleu* candidates, this did not mean that opposition to the Ultramontaines was nonexistent.

The advancement of liberalism against the Church's involvement in politics was not to be easy. As the 36-year-old Wilfrid Laurier put it in 1877, the people were ignorant, the priests "prejudiced and arrogant, and we liberals are put down like enemies of the church, of society, of mankind." Laurier soon began a campaign to convince Quebec that a belief in personal freedom and a steady program of reform by constitutional methods (that being the main basis of political, progressive liberalism) was not necessarily anticlerical or in any way prevented being a good Roman Catholic. In time this courageous stance was to bring him greatness. Meanwhile, clerical influence receded, at least openly, in Quebec politics; the courts disallowed elections because of clerical interference; and Rome announced that the Quebec bishops should exercise a "hands-off" policy toward the Liberal party. By 1877 the Ultramontaine ascendancy was at an end.

The Manitoba schools question involved the nation as a whole and showed the possibilities of cleavage on racial and religious lines. The Manitoba Act (1870) and the Northwest Territories Act (1875) had conferred language and school rights on French and English, Roman Catholic and Protestant alike, throughout the western domains. Theoretically, the French had been given an equal "right of way" for their linguistic and religious expansion in Western Canada. But by 1890, the population there was predominantly Anglo-Saxon and Protestant, and in that year the provincial legislature abolished the denominational system of public education and instituted a scheme which, to all intents and purposes, outlawed French and Roman Catholic schools. In the crisis that raged with great violence for seven years, the sentiment was often voiced that Canada was a British country and as such the French-Canadians should be anglicized. Such statements were made by Dalton McCarthy, a Conservative M.P., the president of the Imperial Federation League, and a spokesman for the so-called Equal Rights Association. On the other side stood French nationalists such as Henri Bourassa, who argued that Confederation could not endure and Canada obtain her full national stature unless "dualism" existed everywhere. English Canada pressed for the principle of majority rule. French Canada supported minority rights. Quebec insisted that remedial legislation be introduced to right the matter. Ontario and Manitoba opposed such a proposal. Ultimately, in 1896, the federal government persuaded the government of Manitoba to grant a concession to the minority: French instruction was to be given where ten students spoke the language. This went a long way to ending the cultural strife of the Manitoba schools question. It would take time before toleration and compromise would grow and mature in Manitoba, and the present racial mosaic there is a testament to that development.

The resolution of the schools question in Manitoba was brought about in part by the change of government in Ottawa in 1896. The Macdonald and Conservative dominance had terminated in that year, and in its stead was that of Laurier and the Liberals. They had failed against Macdonald and the Tories in 1891. In that election, Macdonald, "Old Tomorrow," had claimed that the Liberals were nothing more than annexationists in disguise, that their policy of unrestricted reciprocity with the United States would bring economic ruin and threaten the alliance with Great Britain. With the slogan "The Old Flag, The Old Policy, The Old Leader" the Conservatives won the election.

In 1896, however, the situation was different. Macdonald, his energies spent, had died soon after the 1891 election.[11] Four Tory leaders had failed to fill his shoes and the party was little more than a tattered remnant. As Canada approached the twentieth century, a new ministry was about to bring in policies designed to meet Wilfrid Laurier's prediction, an overly optimistic one as it turned out, that the new century would belong to Canada.

11. "At any rate, after all the excitement of the Reciprocity election was over, Sir John Macdonald, having saved his country from the American danger, as his admirers believed, died a British subject as he had been born a British subject. . . . He was buried in a casket which was imported from West Meriden, Connecticut, and which was an exact facsimile of the casket in which President Garfield of the United States had been buried a short time previously. Well, it is always other Canadians and not ourselves who are liable to be demoralized and de-Canadianized by truck or trade with the Yankees." Underhill, *Image of Confederation*, p. 34.

5

Growing Pains, 1896–1945

The 1896 election marked the beginning of a new era in Canadian history. It was, for one thing, the dawn of a new prosperity. The transformation from a rural, small-town society to an urban industrial country was well underway. It was an age of enterprise, expansion, and exploitation. Fortunes were accumulated by a relatively small number of men whom social critics would later call "the fifty big shots of Canada." "The poor relation has come into her fortune," an English observer noted in 1906, "a single decade has swept away all her diffidence, and has replaced it by a spirit of boundless confidence and booming enterprise." [1]

It was also the start of a period characterized by Canada's growing maturity as a nation. Canada, in the words of the poet Sir Charles G. D. Roberts, was a "child of nations, gianted-limbed." At the head of government stood Wilfrid Laurier, age 55, the first French-Canadian to hold the office of prime minister. Laurier's greatest efforts in the next fifteen years would be devoted to trying to bring Canada's

1. J. A. Hobson, *Canada Today* (London, 1906), p. 4. See also Ramsay Cook, "Stephen Leacock and the Age of Plutocracy, 1903–1921," in John S. Moir, ed., *Character and Circumstances: Essays in Honour of Donald Grant Creighton* (Toronto: Macmillan of Canada, Ltd., 1970), pp. 163–67.

two great races into harmony. At the same time, he wished each to retain its own special qualities, its own viewpoints, its own cultural heritage. He has won his place in national history as the great conciliator, the determined proponent of Canadian national unity and English-French accord.

Yet the Liberal victory of 1896 and the advent of Laurier did not mean a dramatic departure from Conservative policies of preceding decades. The nation might have indeed expected a change in trade policy on the basis of longstanding Liberal policies in favor of reciprocity. But the Liberals chose not to adopt any ill-considered measures, but instead to take into account the interests of the business community and rising sentiment, in Ontario especially, for a preferential tariff in favor of the United Kingdom and against the United States. The result was the 1897 tariff, introduced by the Minister of Finance, W. S. Fielding, which slightly decreased the general level of Canadian protection and promised a reduction of duties of 12½ percent to countries who would reciprocate. In point of fact, this was a general stimulant to Canadian trade with Britain, and so-called "Imperial Preference" was a popular measure at a time when the Dingley tariff in the United States seemed uncompromising to the growth of Canadian-American commerce. Thus the Liberals had kept the essence of the national policy and had modified it to meet the needs of a diversifying, growing economy and of the shifts in American tariff structures.

THE LAST, BEST WEST

At a time when the government was shaping the national policy to new circumstances, Sir Clifford Sifton, the energetic head of the Department of the Interior, was developing policies for peopling that his department described in its immigration pamphlets as the "Last Best West."

Sifton did not wait for immigrants to come. He advertised for them in northern (but not southern) Europe and in the United States, and the rich prairie lands in a prosperous country were his lure. He sought hardy types. To him the stalwart sheepskin-clad peasant of central and eastern Europe was the ideal immigrant, adaptable to the Canadian prairie West. Sifton promoted schemes for assisting the immigrant to get to Quebec City, Montreal, or Halifax and then west to the promised 160 acres—land which under terms of the Dominion Lands Act of 1872 would be owned by the settler after three years of cultivation. An additional quarter section adjoining the initial holding could be available and the final title to the land would be forthcoming if the applicant were a British subject. Sifton tried to keep red tape to a minimum, and with the use of the Northwest Mounted Police extended the rule of law on the prairies in order that the settler would not be faced with lawlessness on the frontier. Sifton's work was also aided by the great land barons of the Canadian West—the Hudson's Bay Company and the Canadian Pacific Railway. The latter was the largest private owner of land in the West, and through pamphlets in many languages, exhibitions, and testimonials, the company advertised for immigrants. The CPR sent lecturers, some of them Canadian farmers, to Britain to promote the settlement scheme and their modes of steamship and railway travel.

The immigrants did not always find Canada as attractive as the promoters' posters or photographs. The transatlantic passage, transcontinental travel, and the final, weary approach to their quarter sections were difficult stages of the journey. Home to them was now good earth in a sea of wild prairie. Where they stopped they searched for whatever wood could be found, built temporary sod houses, dug wells, and tilled the virgin soil. And on the distant horizon, the homesteaders were probably unable to see signs of humanity; isolation and loneliness during winter months induced many to abandon their good land for poorer lands nearer others.

Between 1897 and 1912, 2¼ million persons immigrated to Canada, and a like number would enter the country before 1930. Forty percent of these arrivals were of British stock. Other "new Canadians" came from the United States, Sweden, Finland, Iceland, Russia, Germany, Poland, Holland, or elsewhere. In 1904 Sifton's deputy minister could report, "The steady increase in the flow of immigration that has been directed towards this country, the interest aroused amongst United States capitalists as to its possibilities, the attention which the wealth of its agricultural and other natural resources commands today in Great Britain, in Europe, and even in some of the most important British colonies, clearly shows that Canada has at last emerged from a state of semi-stagnation in which it had remained for so many years, and its future advance, as judged by the remarkable progress of the past few years, must henceforth be by leaps and bounds." Certainly Canada would be a nation of fifteen or twenty millions before a few years. But the Department wanted, or so it claimed, quality more than quantity. They wanted persons of social character such that they would become "loyal, prosperous and contented Canadians." This view constituted the foundations of Canadian immigration policy for the twentieth century.

That these adaptable, proud persons lived in harmony in their adopted land is certain. Many of them left behind religious and political oppressions in Europe, and for them Canada offered new opportunity for cultural interplay. Here one is reminded of the shrewd and saintly Belgian priest of Gabrielle Roy's novel *La petit poule d'eau* (1950)[2] who meditates on the happy mingling of national strains at a northern Manitoba square dance. While to him the old civilization seemed far away, gracious, and kind, at the same time the farther he had come toward the North the freer he had been to love. In this connection, it may be remarked that the Welsh from Patagonia and the Mennonites from Paraguay must surely have been the greatest examples of persons going far northward to the attractions of Canada.

The effect of this immigration on regional agricultural and industrial development was nothing short of dramatic. The agricultural immigrants went especially to the prairies. Accordingly, the population of this region increased from 230,000 in 1891 to 1,327,000 in 1911. The provinces of Alberta and Saskatchewan were created in 1905, an index of their growing populations. Of course, not all of the immigrants were drawn to the soil. In an age of industrial growth, many immigrants (two-thirds of the total, in fact) went to the evolving manufacturing towns as general laborers or mechanics, or became clerks, traders, miners, or navvies working on railroad construction. The good labor supply and the plenitude of jobs gave the nation further reason to be optimistic about its future. At the same time, the buoyant economy camouflaged some urban social ills later brought to the public's attention by the social reformer James Shaver Wood-

2. Translated by Henry Binsse as *Where Nests the Waterhen* (Toronto: New Canadian Library, 1961).

worth and other workers in the Social Gospel movement of the early twentieth century.

Yet another result of this immigration wave was the emergence of another Canada, a Canada whose ethnic makeup could no longer be described as French or British. An observer at the Winnipeg CPR train depot before World War I would have observed the colorful parade of European nationals who had made the western plains their new home. And he would have been right if he had concluded that it would be some decades before these newcomers would gain a facility in English or French. The founding races did not take to the immigrants readily, and sometimes they censured the "Dagoes" or "Bohunks" for not assimilating in an increasingly Anglo-Saxon world. Some newcomers were treated with tolerance and respect; some were not. As long as they accepted the British tradition of law and government in Canada, they would meet with little resistance, and the pressures for conformity were minimal. Some, such as the Hutterites and Doukhobors were exempted from military service. Mormons migrated from Utah to Cardston, Alberta to escape antibigamy laws. Swedes migrated to the Qu'Appelle Valley to overcome depression at home. Remittance men left Britain for the Anglo-Canadian city of Calgary. A racial mosaic with all its complexities existed in Western Canada, and by the mid-twentieth century a new people who were Canadian in a different sense than in, say, Ontario or Quebec had emerged in the West.

The new arrivals would have been impressed by the existing railroads of Canada and by the miles of new track that were being laid. When Laurier and the Liberals took office in 1896, there were many small railways operating in Western Canada, including some developed by those captains of industry, William Mackenzie and Donald Mann. However, the Canadian Pacific Railway was the only transcontinental service. By 1900 the wheat production of the West and the flow of immigrants to the open prairie seemed certain to be without end, and this in turn made another transcontinental feasible. It would also strengthen the national policy and keep trade in Canadian rather than American channels. "We consider that it is the duty of all who sit within these walls by the will of the people," Laurier appealed to Parliament in 1903, "to provide immediate means whereby the products of these new settlers may find an exit to the ocean at the least possible cost and whereby likewise a market may be found in this new region for those who toil in the forests, in the fields, in the mines, in the shops of the older provinces. Such is our duty; it is immediate and imperative."

Laurier was as ambitious as were the railway interests for a second transcontinental. The Grand Trunk Railway wanted to expand westward as the Grand Trunk Pacific. At the same time, the Mackenzie and Mann-owned Canadian Northern Railway hoped to get an eastern outlet for its short roads in the West. In 1903 the government decided to charter the Grand Trunk as a transcontinental railway, appropriately called the National Transcontinental Railway, and gave the company loans and subsidies. This railway, which linked Moncton, New Brunswick, with Prince Rupert, British Columbia, by way of Northern Ontario, Winnipeg, Saskatoon, and Edmonton, was completed in 1915. A third transcontinental, the Canadian Northern, received areas amounting to more than Belgium and Holland combined. It quickly became one of the major railroads of Canada and provided service between Montreal and Vancouver via Winnipeg and Edmonton on track basically north of the Canadian Pacific but south of the National Transcontinental.

Soon the Canadian Northern faced financial difficulties. A brief depression hit the country in 1913 and immigration from Europe ground to a halt with the outbreak of the war in 1914. In 1917 the government took over the line as bankrupt and the Canadian National Railway was born. The country was in possession of a huge railway network far beyond its needs or financial resources. The Grand Trunk Pacific was in a similar financial position and was pulling down the parent Grand Trunk system with it. Its only hope was to get sufficient government funds to operate until the end of the war, when boom times might return. But rising operating costs and the absence of immigration put the railway in a position of bankruptcy. By 1923 the Canadian National Railway had brought the National Transcontinental, the Grand Trunk, the Canadian Northern, and several others under government control. In this crumbling of the private railways only the Canadian Pacific was able to operate with a profit.

It is noteworthy that a private enterprise, the Grand Trunk, rendered an unwitting service to the establishment of Canadian nationalism. A government arbitration board nationalized the Grand

Trunk, refusing to pay the stockholders anything for their stock, which the arbitrators considered to be worthless. The line was controlled by London financiers, and they took the case to court in an attempt to win compensation. The board of the Grand Trunk went so far as to vote themselves a five-year salary before nationalization took effect. The arbitration board held firm and the Grand Trunk was finally taken over by the Canadian government; not, however, before the Canadian public became aroused by the flagrant tactics of the British directors of the Grand Trunk. Just as before, when American financial interests forced the Canadians to watch that country with suspicion, during the Grand Trunk arbitration, Canadians began to observe British capitalists with a certain amount of animosity. The railways had made a further, subtle contribution to Canadian nationalism.

For King and Country

The Laurier years witnessed perhaps one of the greatest debates in Canadian history on the question of Canada's participation in British imperial affairs. Simply put, the issue involved the degree to which Canada should contribute to the foreign policy and defense of the British Empire. Canadian historians have divided the opposing camps in English Canada into the "nationalists" and the "imperialists." Often the differences were slight or even nonexistent.[3] The nationalists included the lawyer John S. Ewart who, until his death in 1899, advocated Canadian independence under the British Crown; John W. Dafoe, editor of the *Manitoba Free Press,* who through his writings influenced a whole generation of press gallery members and reporters; and J. D. Edgar, a Liberal M.P., who argued that French-Canadians could contribute to national strength. The "nationalists" were countered by the so-called "imperialists." One such was Principal George Munro Grant of Queen's University, who earlier in his *Ocean to Ocean* (1873) had written that independence for 4 million Cana-

3. There are numerous works on this subject, but the reader's attention is directed to Carl Berger's *Sense of Power: Studies in the Ideas of Canadian Imperialism, 1867–1914* (Toronto: University of Toronto Press, 1970), which explains how some Canadians regarded national independence as not being incompatible with cooperation with the British Empire.

dians face to face with 38 million Americans was an impossibility. Canada, he said, could best fulfil her destiny through the British Empire. Sir Sandford Fleming, the railway engineer, Colonel George T. Denison, one of the original members of Canada First and an advocate of imperial federation, and Sir George Parkin, some-time Principal of Upper Canada College and after 1902 administrator of the Rhodes Trust, all saw identification with the Empire as the safeguard for Canadians, a fulfilment of their destiny. Stephen Leacock, another, put it this way: "To many people in Canada, this imperialism is a tainted word. It is too much associated with a truckling subservience to English people and English ideas and the silly swagger of the hop-o'-my-thumb junior officer. But there is and must be for the future of our country, a higher and more real imperialism than this—the imperialism of the plain man at the plough and the clerk in the counting house, the imperialism of any decent citizen that demands for this country its proper place in the councils of the Empire and in the destiny of the world. In this sense, imperialism means but the realization of a Greater Canada, the recognition of a wider citizenship. I, that write these lines, am an Imperialist because I will not be a Colonial." [4]

This conflict of "nationalists" and "imperialists" was bitter and divisive. In an age when European imperialism was reaching its zenith, the relationship of French Canada with English Canada and the Empire as a whole prohibited an easy course of action for the Dominion. Actually, the Dominion's position was already defined. In 1885 Sir John A. Macdonald would not send Canadian troops to the Sudan because, as he said, England was not at war and Canadian "men and money would therefore be sacrificed to get Gladstone and Co. out of the hole they have plunged themselves into by their own imbecility." His contemporary, the Quebec Premier Honoré Mercier, had opposed the imperial federationists because he believed they would send French-Canadians off to bloody and distant wars over which Canada had no control. This myth, in many ways unfounded, was maintained by Henri Bourassa, the most notable of the French-Canadian nationalists of the Laurier era, who quit the Liberal party

4. Stephen Leacock, "Greater Canada: An Appeal," *The University Magazine*, VI (June 1907), 132.

in 1899. He argued, incorrectly, that Canada's role in the South African war had resulted from Laurier's collaboration with the Colonial Office and the Canadian imperialists. By 1903 he had formed the *Ligue Nationaliste* to fight British imperialism and promote Canadian neutrality. The anti-imperialist strain in French-speaking Quebec was strong, so much so that it is not surprising that Laurier had to follow compromise policies agreeable to nationalists and imperialists. His view that Canada should shape her own destiny in the world met with little resistance.

Laurier's first opportunity to develop his country's position in the Empire came in 1897 with the celebration of Queen Victoria's Diamond Jubilee. This testament to the greatness of the queen, her sixty-year reign, and her vast dominions overseas brought colonial prime ministers and soldiers to London for the pageant. Laurier was there and so were the North West Mounted Police in their scarlet tunics. Joseph Chamberlain, the Secretary of State for the Colonies, proposed closer imperial relations in political, economic, and military matters. But he met with resistance from the colonial premiers, who feared imperial centralization at the expense of colonial autonomy. Nonetheless, Laurier—now Sir Wilfrid—returned to Canada with an appreciation for the needs of greater imperial cooperation at a time when shifting European alliances and rising imperalist states cast lengthy shadows over certain quarters of the British Empire.[5] Canada would cooperate with the empire—in trade, defense, and communications—but not be led by it.

By this time, Canada had already awakened to the dangers of this precarious state of affairs. In 1895 American thrusts for primacy in the Western Hemisphere had ominous implications for Canada. In particular, the Venezuela-British Guiana boundary dispute revealed that the United States might prevent any permanent political union between any European power and its American possessions. Britain's acquiescence to American demands and, in 1901, her withdrawal from a joint interest with the United States in the projected

5. As he said at the Imperial Institute in London in June 1897, "If a day were ever to come when England was in danger, let the bugle sound, let the fires be lighted on the hills, and in all parts of the colonies, though we might not be able to do much, whatever we can do shall be done by the colonies to help her." In August 1914, as the House of Commons *Debates* testify, his view was the same.

Panama Canal were further evidence of the collapse of the *Pax Britannica*. How could Canada fare in future developments? These manifestations of American imperialism augured poorly for Canada.

The Alaska boundary dispute gave Canadians further evidence that they were party to a shifting balance of power over which they had no control. In 1896 gold fever, so ably described in Pierre Berton's *Klondike*, broke out in the Yukon. Most of the gold was to be found on Canadian soil, and could only be reached by crossing the Alaska panhandle, the eastern limits of which were still in doubt. United States and British conventions with Russia in 1824 and 1825 respectively did not define this boundary with any accuracy and by purchasing Russian America in 1867, the United States inherited all Russian claims in America. The United States wanted to gain as much territory as possible, apparently without regard to the interests of her neighbor. Canada also wanted territory—territory that would give her coastal access on the Pacific north of 54°40′ North latitude. Canadian newspapers and Laurier assumed an anti-American stance that did not go unnoticed in the American press. A *New York Herald* cartoon depicted Canada as a young girl pulling feathers from the tail of the American eagle and Uncle Sam is seen saying to John Bull: "If the small person is not restrained the eagle may lose his temper."

The boundary question lapsed during the Boer War. Britain, perhaps under some obligation to back Canada in turn for her help in South Africa, expected American acquiescence in turn for giving the United States full rights to build a Panama canal. But Theodore Roosevelt would hear nothing of this. He considered the Canadian claim to be as exaggerated as if Canada claimed the island of Nantucket. Determined to use his "big stick" to get a settlement favorable to his country, in March 1902 he dispatched orders to send troops to Alaska. He also proposed a mixed tribunal consisting of "six impartial jurists of repute" which would review the matter. The Americans were Elihu Root, the secretary of war who had dispatched the troops to Alaska; George Turner, a Washington state senator violently opposed to concessions to Canada; and Henry Cabot Lodge, who had publicly condemned the Canadian case. The Canadian representatives, who were perhaps no less disinterested in the nation's claim, were Sir Louis Jetté, Lieutenant-Governor of Quebec, and A. B. Aylesworth, a Toronto lawyer. The third man in the British-Canadian delegation was none other than the Lord Chief Justice of England, Lord Alverstone.

On October 20, 1903, the Alaska Boundary Tribunal brought down its decision in favor of the American case. Alverstone had sided with the United States representatives, and it is now well known that the British government, owing to American pressure and the need for preserving Anglo-American accord, may have, as Roosevelt brazenly stated later, "tipped the wink" to Alverstone.

The settlement of the Alaska dispute revived Canadian suspicions of the United States and Britain. The villains of the story are Chamberlain, the fickle colonial secretary, and Lord Alverstone, the traitorous judge. Such an interpretation fails to take into consideration the fact that the *Pax Britannica* was at an end, and that in the circumstances Great Britain had at stake international considerations of greater moment than the possession of a remote coastline and access by sea to the Yukon goldfields. Nonetheless, the dispute was a great Canadian lesson in international diplomacy. Henceforth Canada would aim to act in her own interests whenever she could. Of necessity, she was coming of age, and the process was painful.

Anglo-American accord over the Alaska boundary comprised part of a movement toward a *rapprochement* between the two powers, and this alignment of English-speaking peoples gave Canada free security. Laurier admitted in 1902 that the Monroe Doctrine guaranteed Canadian defense. Canadian-American relations quickly improved. In 1909 the International Joint Commission was established to deal with border questions. Since that time it has functioned as a body dedicated to the principle that the two countries can resolve their differences without war or the fear of war. In 1910, the International Court settled the longstanding Atlantic fisheries question in favor of Canada. The neighbors were learning to live in harmony. Canadians began to forget their ancient fears of American attack and, at the same time, American aspirations for continental dominion seemed to diminish. But they did not disappear, as the 1911 election would show.

Meanwhile, in intra-imperial affairs, Canada became embroiled in the Boer War despite the reluctance of the Quebec nationalists to support what appeared to be, at first glance, a British imperial adventure in faraway lands where Canadian security was not directly threatened. At the beginning of the conflict, Laurier sought to maintain the delicate balance of national unity by resisting the pressures of Lord Minto, the governor-general, and of Major-General E. T. Hutton, the general officer commanding the militia, that a contingent be sent to South Africa. But at bottom, Canada was a British nation and British defeats during the early stages of the war, especially during November 1899, changed matters. Britain asked for assistance and English Canada demanded that troops be sent. Laurier acquiesced, and 7,500 volunteers, including a cavalry regiment raised at Lord Strathcona's expense, crossed the Atlantic to the Cape. On the veldt they fought "as soldiers of the Queen" beside fellow subjects from New Zealand, Australia, Britain, and elsewhere. This armed partnership of British nations marked the beginning of a wartime alliance that would be reenacted in 1914 and again in 1939.

The government's decision to go to war was taken on behalf of the nation and in support of the Empire. In future, as Laurier proclaimed in 1900, Canada would continue to be at liberty to act or not to act in wars. At the Colonial Conference of 1902 he encouraged trade preferences within the Empire, a theme taken up by the Colonial Secretary, Joseph Chamberlain, but with little success. But Laurier opposed all proposals for imperial solidarity in defense and government. Such a departure from the nation's unannounced policy of minimizing international commitments would endanger the sensitive interplay of French and English in Canada. The nation was indeed, as the French observer Siegfried stated in 1906, a "precarious creation." And Laurier trod uncertain ground in search of political security.

Laurier, nonetheless, found it increasingly difficult to walk the middle ground, for the delicate question of naval defense was taking on added meaning as new powers rose to challenge the Empire's primacy. By 1890 the growing disparity between British and United States naval forces on the North American and Pacific stations meant that the British had no means of supporting their diplomacy. Accord with the United States became essential and this had important ramifications for Canada. So too did the Anglo-Japanese Alliance of 1902, which gave added security to parts of the British Empire within the Pacific rim, including British Columbia. Under these new circumstances Halifax and Esquimalt ceased in 1905 to be station headquarters for British fleets in North American and Pacific waters, and in 1910 and 1911, respectively, these shore establishments were transferred to Canadian control. British warships were withdrawn to home waters to counter the growing German navy, and new battleships of the Dreadnought class were built to safeguard the communications, trade, and security of not only the British Isles but the outlying ports of the Empire, including Canada. The British government believed that the Empire should share in the costs of this defense. Laurier and the Liberals disagreed. Their argument, based on the principle that Canada would decide when and how it would contribute, aimed at giving Canada as much freedom to act as possible. It goes without saying that Canada, at no cost to herself, was now being protected by British alliances with Japan and the United States, and of course by British military power itself.

As an alternative, Canada acquired, somewhat reluctantly, a navy. The Canadian Naval Service Act of 1910 established the organizational force for the Royal Canada Navy. Two obsolete cruisers—"one for each ocean"—were purchased from Britain for training purposes. But no new ships of any strength were added to the Canada "fleet." In 1914, incidentally, British Columbia hurriedly bought two submarines to shore up her sagging defenses against a seemingly imminent attack from a German cruiser, and these were later added to the Canadian force. These were token gestures. The nation failed to understand the shifts in power on the international stage that Canada was so anxious to enter. Her sister dominions, Australia and New Zealand, not yet under the protection of the United States, each contributed the costs of building one Dreadnought. But Canada rejected the Admiralty's request for one battleship, three cruisers, six destroyers, and three submarines as her share to the Royal Navy. Canada's "tin pot navy" of 1910 was symbolically representative of the government's attention to national unity and autonomy.

Laurier's plan to build a Canadian navy instead of aiding the Royal Navy with monies or ships cost him considerable support in the 1911 election. The naval question was perhaps less important than that of reciprocity, but in a way the two hinged around the same issue—whether Canada should favor closer relations with the United States or with Britain and the Empire. Laurier, under pressures from the Canadian Council of Agriculture, reached agreement with the

United States government for virtually unrestricted reciprocity. This agreement would have to be ratified by the governments of both countries. In Washington, the Democrats, who traditionally favored free trade, gave consent. But in Ottawa, the proposal met with obstruction from the manufacturing, railway, and banking interests, including eighteen Toronto Liberals and the Conservatives. Laurier had no option but to "go to the country" in an election, and Parliament dissolved.

In the 1911 campaign, the Conservatives focused their attention on loyalty. As their 57-year-old leader, Robert Laird Borden, put it in his electoral appeal, "Let us never forget that Canada cannot become fiscally and commercially part of the United States and remain politically a part—and an important part—of the British Empire." "We must decide," he stressed, "whether the spirit of Canadianism or of continentalism shall prevail on the northern half of the continent."

The Conservatives, using the slogan "No truck or trade with the Yankees," carried the day. It is no less significant that they had been helped by tactless speeches of American politicians and newspapermen favoring annexation. Canadians had identified reciprocity with continentalism, and in a spirit of independence rejected commercial union. As for the Liberals, their change of policy toward free trade in a time of prosperity was perhaps unnecessary and foolish. Reflecting on the wounds of his defeat, one Liberal wrote to another, "I am neither laughing nor weeping—I am just thinking—what damn fools we were." Thus did the fifteen-year Liberal era come to an end.

That the new government's speech from the throne in 1911 contained no reference to the naval question is not surprising. Borden wanted to reconsider the relation of Dominion to Empire. In 1912, his plan to make a direct contribution of $35 million to provide the Grand Fleet with three battleships was stated in a new naval bill. Under this scheme, the Borden government was prepared to take on burdens in imperial defense, provided it received a voice in the direction of imperial policy. In this sense Borden was a nationalist prepared to make imperial commitments and thereby assert the unused military potential of Canada. Ironically, Borden's naval bill miscarried. It did not pass the Senate, where the Liberals held the majority, and before a revised plan could be framed and enough Conservatives appointed to the upper chamber to stop Liberal obstruction, Canada was at war.

On August 4, 1914, Britain was at war with Germany and so was Canada.

The First World War

The year 1914 brought a remote Dominion, previously secure behind the walls of British sea power and the Monroe Doctrine, into the quarrels of Europe. Canada had entered the world stage. No longer could the fledgling nation avoid sharing in Britain's heavy responsibilities. Legally, of course, she was at war against the German and Austro-Hungarian empires as soon as Britain declared war. But whether or not she fought was up to the Canadian government. This was Laurier's idea of Empire and Borden's too. The German invasion of Belgium convinced most factions in Canada of Germany's designs, and all parties—Conservatives, Liberals, and Quebec Nationalists—joined in the crusade "to make the world safe for democracy." Laurier endorsed Canada's actions in support of Britain. It was time, he said, for Canadians to accept the responsibilities and sacrifices of British citizenship. Bourassa, the nationalist, announced that he would support the sending of Canadian troops to Europe in order to assist "the combined efforts of England and France." The press also voiced unanimity in the case. Few voices spoke against Canada's position in the war.

At the commencement of hostilities there was no trouble getting volunteers for the Canadian armed forces. By October, the first Canadian contingent had reached England, and by late 1915, some 212,000 Canadians were under arms. By the end of the war this number had grown to 619,636 men in the army alone. This was 7½ percent of the national population. About 24,000 joined the Royal Flying Corps, where they comprised about a quarter of the pilots. Among them was the fighter ace, "Billy" Bishop, who shot down 72 enemy planes. In addition, some 8,000 enlisted in the Royal Canadian Navy, and by 1918 there were 134 small warships in commission. Almost overnight a basically unmilitary people had gone wholeheartedly into war.

In Ottawa, meanwhile, the government passed legislation designed to give it ample powers to direct the national effort. The War Measures Act of 1914, later invoked in 1939 and again in 1970 (during civil disturbances in Quebec), and the War Appropriations Act increased the federal government's role in directing the economy, increasing the armed forces and controlling the movements of persons. War stimulated the economy. Munitions production grew to such a degree that 30 percent of all British shells were made in Canada. The pulp and paper industry grew quickly. Mineral production—in copper, lead, zinc, and nickel—expanded. Agricultural production, especially in grains, developed rapidly, and in 1917 a Board of Grain Supervisors was established to market shipments.

The war brought large profits to the manufacturers and primary producers, and this did not go unnoticed. N. A. Rowell, the leader of the Ontario Liberal party, charged that Canada "profited the most and suffered the least . . . of any of the nations of the Empire." With New Zealand and Australia contributing proportionally more manpower and less economic production to the war than Canada, this allegation was well-founded. In Canada, the war brought prosperity and an end to Canada's adverse trade balance; it also brought the income tax and Victory Loans in 1917. It also brought half-hearted attempts at rationing and cost of living controls. The ineffectiveness of the Cost of Living Commissioner, the Food Controller, and the War Trade Board was bound to cause domestic discontent and augment the already existing economic disparities in Canadian society. By 1918 the nation lingered on the threshold of economic uncertainty and, in the following year, in Winnipeg, social discontent developed into a general strike. The government, through the office of the Minister of Justice, Arthur Meighen, employed measures to keep "peace, order and good government." In an era when the Bolshevik revolution loomed large in the Western world, it is not surprising to find the government supporting Big Business at the expense of the youthful labor movement. This was a legacy of war.

Another effect of the war was national disunity. A nation that had entered the war on a unified basis by 1917 found itself torn asunder by racial tensions. In Ontario, Regulation 17 sought to control the teaching of French, and understandably French-Canadians looked on this step of anglicization with suspicion. They were further angered by claims from English-Canadians that French Canada was not supplying men for the army as it ought to. French-Canadian enlistments were indeed low by 1916, and the foolhardy efforts of the anti-French Minister of Militia and Defence, Colonel Sir Sam Hughes, did nothing to soothe their uneasiness. From the English-Canadian pulpits came cries that French Canada was not doing its share. At the same time, from Europe came reports that there were more casualties than enlistments in the Canadian army.

Borden, by this time a member of the Imperial War Cabinet and thus clearly aware of the Allied manpower needs, believed in the necessity of conscription. Only by the draft could enough recruits be brought into the armed forces to meet the needs on the Western Front. The battles of Ypres, the Somme, Passchendael, and Vimy Ridge brought heavy losses to the Canadians; and the gas, mud, and bloodshed of the Western Front helped Canada come of age. But how could this be done at home where Laurier would not accept Borden's invitation to unite in the common cause? Laurier believed that to accept would be to give over control of French Canada to Bourassa and the nationalists. Accordingly, Borden and some Liberals, including Sifton and Rowell, brought in the Military Service Bill after they had formed the Union government in October 1917 and had won a federal election in December. The Unionists swept English Canada with 150 seats. Laurier and his followers dominated Quebec with 62 seats but held only 20 elsewhere. The election results made two things clear: first, that conscription had divided the country; second, that French Canada had become isolated from the rest of the nation. The costs of conscription to national unity were great, and the 120,000 men subsequently raised did not bring the Army up to its desired strength.

In the overseas war effort, Borden opposed committing a large number of Canadian troops to British military leadership. He resisted British plans to integrate the imperial forces, and he insisted on a role in the making of war policies. He organized a Canadian general staff and, accordingly, in 1917 General Sir Arthur Currie replaced General Sir Julian Byng (later Lord Byng of Vimy) as officer commanding the Canadian Corps. With General Jan Smuts of South Africa, Borden sat on the Imperial War Cabinet and at the Imperial War Conference in 1917 he introduced a resolution calling for a reappraisal of dominion status after the war. As he saw it, Canada and the other self-governing nations of the British Empire ought to have autonomy in domestic affairs and an equal voice in foreign policy.

After the war, Borden continued as a proponent of Canada's right to be heard in the councils of the world. He believed the dominions, as separate entities, should sign the peace treaties at Paris and they did, under the general category "British Empire." Canada also became a member of the League of Nations, with a seat in the League Assembly and the International Labor Organization. When in July 1920 Borden resigned because of poor health, it could be fairly said that he had given Canada a new status in the world. Devoted to Crown and Country, his statesmanlike policies promoted Canadian maturity in the troubled international relations of the twentieth century.

Social Discontent in the Aftermath of War

In the aftermath of war, some Canadians sought a reappraisal of their national role. The "war to end war," the war to uphold Western civilization, left a bad taste in the mouths of women, soldiers, and laborers. This was partially disguised by flappers, touring cars, and the light entertainment of the twenties. Below this facade of pleasure lay economic and social conditions in need of reform. Universal franchise, established by Parliament in 1920, gave the vote to all male and female citizens 21 years of age. But discrimination against women being employed was strong: the spinster teacher was a typical employee of school boards who would not hire married women.

Among men, also, there was reason for complaint. The Winnipeg general strike of 1919, already mentioned, had shown the discontent of labor and the government's preference for supporting Big Business. The needs for urban reform and an end to poverty, as seen before the war by James Shaver Woodsworth at All Peoples' Mission in Winnipeg, and described in his book *My Neighbour*, published in 1911, persisted after 1918. This son of Methodist moralism continued with others such as Salem Bland to work toward the eradication of urban ills. Their efforts were part of a wider North American and European movement. They took the church to the streets and the streets to the church. Sometimes they met theological resistance; in Woodsworth's case, he believed that only by becoming a member of Parliament, which he did in 1921, could he attract the nation's attention to the existing social dislocation. They developed or were aided by temperance unions, various Christian associations, the Lord's Day Alliance, and moral and social councils. Sometimes they were helped by sympathetic officials at the federal, provincial, and municipal level who saw the need to reshape Canadian society.[6]

At the same time that reformers were at work in the city, others were at work on the farms, especially in the West. In November 1918 the Canadian Council of Agriculture called for a "new national policy" to reduce tariffs and freight rates and the prices of agricultural machinery and to promote trade. The government did not respond, and the economic collapse of 1919 and 1920 caused farmers to demonstrate en masse. They formed United Farmers parties and between 1919 and 1922 they carried the elections in Ontario, Alberta, and Manitoba. They also inspired a new national party, the Progressives, led by Thomas A. Crerar. So great was the agriculturalist movement that in the election of 1921 the Progressives sent 64 members to Ottawa.[7]

The Progressives came chiefly from the West, and they represented sectional discontent. With the Liberals holding almost all of the 65 Quebec seats and most of those in the Maritimes, and with the Conservatives dominating in Ontario and British Columbia, it is fair to say that in 1921 sectionalism had replaced the racialism arising out of the Conscription crisis of 1917.

The Conservatives were led by Arthur Meighen, a man despised by French Canada and labor. He had replaced Borden as prime minister in 1920. His party's poor showing in 1921 can be attributed partly to his uncompromising stands against labor and opponents of conscription. That his pro-Empire leanings contributed to his unpopularity seems plausible.

Meighen's political rival was William Lyon Mackenzie King, grandson of the rebel William Lyon Mackenzie. This semi-intellectual, spiritualist Liberal had remained loyal to Laurier in 1917 on the conscription issue and in 1921 he became prime minister. Lacking personal charm and oratorical skills, he was nonetheless a man of great political ability, and he ran up a record as first minister that exceeded Walpole's longevity in the early eighteenth century. From 1921 to

6. See Richard Allen, *The Social Passion: Religion and Social Reform in Canada, 1914–28* (Toronto: University of Toronto Press, 1971).

7. The election of 1921 returned 116 Liberals, 64 Progressives, 50 Conservatives, and 5 others.

1945 he was perhaps the most important man in Canada; and he was prime minister for all of this time except for a brief period in 1926 and again in 1930–1935. His and his party's policies, both domestic and foreign, were controversial and of a longstanding significance.

The social policy of Mackenzie King and the Liberals during the 1920s was to "let sleeping dogs lie." He could only do this because the country experienced an economic boom reminiscent of the Laurier years. The forests of the Precambrian Shield contained the water-power, minerals, and pulpwoods for this new expansion; and Canada's vision turned toward the North and the South. Trade increased with both the United Kingdom and the United States. However, after 1925, exports to the United States exceeded those to Britain, and in the twenties Americans invested about $2.5 billion in Canada, either in equity investments or branch plants. Meanwhile, British investments, which had been chiefly in bonds used for Canadian enterprises, public and private, declined. Canada drew closer to the American economic orbit while Mackenzie King and the Liberals did nothing to prevent Wall Street from controlling St. James Street in Montreal or Bay Street in Toronto. When the crash came in 1929, Canada's economy as a resource supplier for American industry was perforce hard-hit. In external affairs the Liberals were similarly shifting their preference toward the Americans. They did so at the expense of imperial affinities.

Imperial Relations in the Postwar World

It has been fairly said that in this period Britain did not wish to embroil the Dominions in war without their consent, and at the same time that the Dominions did not want "to be dragged into a war at Britain's coat-tails." [8] But Mackenzie King, the Liberals, and the Liberal press did not always see it that way. In point of fact, there could be no unity to Empire foreign policy because of colonial nationalism that existed in varying degrees and forms in Canada, South Africa, Australia, and New Zealand. In the Chanak Crisis, for instance, Mackenzie King would not meet Britain's appeal for assistance in uphold-

8. J. D. B. Miller, *Britain and the Old Dominions* (London: Chatto and Windus, 1966), p. 111.

ing Greek interests in the face of Turkish advances in Anatolia in 1922. He said that the Canadian Parliament would have to be summoned to authorize such action and that he had no desire to call Parliament. "No advance commitments" became his way of conducting Anglo-Canadian affairs and he was true to a policy that had been in existence since Macdonald's day.

Although Meighen and the Conservatives would have been more sympathetic to British requests and could have done so on a legitimate Canadian basis, Mackenzie King and the Liberals shied away from world commitments. For instance, Canada did not sign the Geneva Protocol of 1924 which made aggression an international crime. Canada, members of the government declared, wanted to be on her own and uncommitted. As Senator Raoul Dandurand, a delegate to the League of Nations Assembly, put it, Canada could be likened to "a fire-proof house, far from inflammable materials."

North American affairs were a different matter for here, of course, Canada had a direct interest. In 1920 Canada acquired from Britain the right to appoint a minister in Washington, and this right was exercised in 1927 when Vincent Massey was appointed to the post. His reception in Washington suggests how little Americans knew about Canada at the time.[9] In 1921, under Meighen's government, Canada was influential in ending the Anglo-Japanese alliance and thereby increasing Anglo-American accord and, in turn, providing Canada with protection free from Japanese influence. In 1923, Canada negotiated and signed the Halibut Treaty with the United States, the first treaty signed by the dominion independently of the United Kingdom.

These developments have sometimes been taken to mean that Canadians were taking great steps forward in their search for autonomy. They were actually representative of an isolationist nation, tired of war, trying to deal with continental affairs. Having cut the apron strings which bound them voluntarily to Mother, they were now responsible for all the housework. In all these developments, Britain did not hinder Canada and the other Dominions in seeking control of their own domestic and foreign affairs in the uncertain times after World War I.

9. See Vincent Massey, *What's Past is Prologue* (Toronto: Macmillan Company of Canada, 1963), p. 123. Canadian ambassadors were appointed to Paris in 1928 and Tokyo in 1929.

The Chanak Crisis, already considered, has frequently been regarded as an attempt by Britain to coerce the Dominions in matters of foreign affairs. Another event that has been dwelled upon as proof of British "interference" in Canadian affairs is the constitutional struggle between Mackenzie King and the Governor-General, Viscount Byng of Vimy. When Byng rejected Mackenzie King's request for dissolution of Parliament after the government had been defeated on June 26, 1926, chaos broke out in Ottawa. Meighen formed a government momentarily but on July 2 it was voted as illegal on the grounds that the governor-general had rejected Parliament's advice. In the ensuing election, the Liberals argued that Byng's refusal to dissolve Parliament was unconstitutional, while the Conservatives emphasized the details of the customs scandal that had brought the Liberals down in the first place. Byng did not appear in a favorable light. If anything, the press saw him as interfering in Canadian affairs. The election returned Mackenzie King and the Liberals to power with a small working majority.

Thus a definition of the governor-general's role was in order, and in 1926 the Imperial Conference declared that he was a representative of the Crown and not of the British government. He would serve in the same capacity in the Dominion as the monarch in relation to his ministers at Westminster. The conference went even further. Henceforth, any Empire treaty action would not necessarily bind the individual dominions in foreign affairs. The Balfour declaration, which came from the conference, adopted the following as the principle of future intra-imperial affairs: The Dominions "are autonomous communities within the British Empire, equal in status, in no way subordinate one to another in any aspect of their domestic or external affairs, though united by a common allegiance to the Crown, and freely associated as members of the British Commonwealth of Nations."

This declaration of flexibility has been considered mistakenly in Canada as a great landmark in Canadian autonomy. Really, however, it was defining the already existing practices of the Anglo-Canadian relationship. The Statute of Westminster of 1931 set them down in statutory form. The evolutionary growth of British governmental practice in the various self-governing parts of the British Empire are a distinct feature of modern history: Canada contributed to this process and was one of the beneficiaries. By 1931 then, it could be safely said that Canada had acquired a new status among the nations of the world. Another vestige of her colonial status had disappeared. However, she still continued as a North American member of the British family of nations, linked by filial ties and sentiment to Britain but motivated by North American influences. In this regard she was very much part of what the great historian, John Bartlett Brebner, called the "North Atlantic triangle." These influences would shape the future course of Canadian history.

The Dirty Thirties

On October 24, 1929, Wall Street shook with economic uncertainty. The stock market crash ushered in a decade or more of financial dislocation in Canada. The Depression was unprecedented in both length and degree; and Canada's economic function as a world supplier of raw materials, grains, and pulp and paper was disrupted by the collapse of overseas markets as tariffs rose in the U.S., Europe, and Japan. As Blair Neatby has written, the Depression reinforced "the need for new national policies. It aggravated some of the social cleavages already emerging, it made many of the grievances more acute, and it influenced the choice of political priorities. It is in this sense that the decade of the 1930s is both the end of one era and the beginning of another. It marks the concern with the problems with which we are still painfully familiar." [10] Depression became a state of mind. Stability and security were absent. Society and social institutions were on trial. Accepted values in economic and political life were questioned. As a result, new concepts of the role of government emerged as well as the creation of new parties and institutions. Such were "The Politics of Chaos."

The Depression was the biggest job that governments of the interwar period had to face. Mackenzie King, who had the first chance to alleviate the problems confronting the Canadians, did little. Confused by events, he had nothing constructive to offer. The demands of the provinces for relief and unemployment schemes were given short hearing by Mackenzie King. He went on record as saying he would

10. H. Blair Neatby, *The Politics of Chaos: Canada in the Thirties* (Toronto: Macmillan of Canada, 1972), p. 41.

not give a five-cent piece to any Conservative government in the provinces because their policies were opposed to Ottawa. Such unsympathetic response did him no good, and with the Conservatives gaining in provincial elections, the mood of the nation turned against King. "He blunted us," wrote F. R. Scott in his poem W.L.M.K. "He skilfully avoided what was wrong/ Without saying what was right,/ And never let his on the one hand/ Know what his on the other hand was doing . . ." While the prime minister vacillated, the Wheat Pool collapsed, some railways came to a stop, and the primary producers went broke. Not surprisingly, R. B. Bennett's Conservatives returned 137 members to Ottawa in 1931. The Liberals, with 88 seats, had been rejected. There were 20 "others."

In Richard Bedford Bennett the nation hoped to find the superman to redress the economic faults of the times. A successful lawyer and businessman, and the inheritor of the E. B. Eddy Match Company fortune, he was in the public's eye, the embodiment of prosperity. But he dominated his cabinet, so much so that it was joked by newsmen that if Bennett were seen talking to himself as he walked alone on Parliament Hill this was his version of holding a cabinet meeting. In the end, his superman characteristics were to betray him, and in this respect he was similar to some other national leaders of his time.

Bennett acted quickly to counteract the Depression, to relieve unemployment or "perish in the attempt." Parliament voted $20 million in September 1930 for unemployment relief and public works projects. It passed the Unemployment and Farm Relief Bill in 1931, and created the Canadian Broadcasting Corporation in 1932 and the Bank of Canada, as a private organization, in 1934. It also supported an increase in the national tariff. In 1932, at the Imperial Economic Conference in Ottawa, Canada and Britain signed an agreement of mutual trade preference. For Bennett, these policies represented his policy of "Canada First and then the Empire." These measures served to give some shelter to Canadian manufacturing and provide some protection for primary producers.

But on the farms and in the towns and cities, signs of the Depression were everywhere. Drifted soil, abandoned farmhouses, and "Bennett buggies"—automobiles drawn by horses—typified the poverty of the Prairie provinces. After the bumper crop of 1928, wheat-growing regions often became dust bowls. In parts of Saskatchewan, not a drop of rain fell for two and a half years. Younger sons left the farms to ride the rails from city to city in search of employment. Teachers and doctors went on relief, and school children suffered. Cases existed in which children would go to school every other day; because two children had only one set of clothes between them, one would go to school while the other would stay in bed. Some schools were closed because school boards could not pay fuel bills. Unemployment relief camps, soup kitchens, and food allowance schemes became the order of the day. In these circumstances, the morale and general attitudes of those who suffered most was tested: not surprisingly many persons ended formerly productive lives on "skid row" as bums, beggars, pimps, and prostitutes. The empty freight car symbolized the national tragedy.

By 1935, one-tenth of the nation was on relief, and the social dislocation of the times led over a thousand men to "trek" by road and rail from Vancouver eastward to Ottawa. The object of the On-to-Ottawa trek was to force Bennett to listen to demands for work and wages. About the time the trekkers reached Regina, Bennett was receiving eight representatives of the trek in Ottawa. The interview revealed the prime minister's fears that constitutional authority might be endangered. Slim Evans, the group spokesman, objected to Bennett's charge that the men were not wanting any work. "Give any of us work and see whether we will work," was his reply. "This is an insidious attempt to propagandize the press on your part, and anybody who professes to be Premier and uses such despicable tactics is not fit to be premier of a Hottentot village."

Despite these demands, Bennett held firm to his convictions that his national relief programs were working, that a Bolshevik revolution was in the offing, and that the government was aware of the seriousness of the situation. The trek was halted at Regina by his order that they could not proceed eastward by the unlawful use of railway transportation. For the trekkers, confrontation politics had been unsuccessful. For the government, Bennett's position had been enhanced. In time new institutions were created to provide economic stability. The greatest activity was in social welfare, family allowances, old-age pensions, unemployment, and medicare. These policies were all attempts to reduce insecurity in an industrial society.

The Depression gave birth to new political creeds. Perhaps the most important of these was the Cooperative Commonwealth Federation, or C.C.F. As early as 1904 the Socialist Party of Canada had been formed, and during the Winnipeg General Strike the socialist cause won a few adherents and not a few enemies. Woodsworth, its leader, believed that democratic socialism along British lines would minimize the evils of capitalism. The Depression gave impetus to Woodsworth's movement. In 1932, in Calgary, representatives of farmers' groups, labor, and the university community formed the C.C.F. In the next year their Regina Manifesto announced the party's objective: "We aim to replace the capitalist system, with its inherent injustice and inhumanity, by a social order from which the domination and exploitation of one class by another, will be eliminated." A government-planned economy was the C.C.F.'s policy for bringing economic equality, and under this policy the railways, insurance companies, banks, and major industries would come under government ownership or regulation.

Another outgrowth of western discontent in the 1930s was "Social Credit." Based on the political views of Major C. H. Douglas, an English engineer, it advanced a movement against the control of capital by the "fifty big shots of Canada." Its leader in Canada, "Bible Bill" Aberhart, a school teacher and fundamentalist minister of the Prophetic Bible Institute, was a skillful speaker. His Sunday church sermons, heard on the radio in Alberta, told of how a "social credit" of $25 a month would be paid to citizens. By government regulation, a "just price" could be determined, purchasing power would rise, and poverty could be minimized. His appeal for economic justice won the support of Alberta farmers. One of them later recalled: "Us farmers, being the producers of real wealth, were the first to feel the pinch and we felt it the hardest as the years went by. When we were all feeling down and out, Mr. Aberhart began to show the link between the economic injustices of today and the economic injustices of Christ's time. He linked these two up and showed how Christ had cleared the money changers out of the Temple. Then he showed us how the money changers of today had everything cornered . . . the tie-up between religion and economics made me realize that Social Credit was the answer to all our problems. Once I realized this, I went out and talked up Social Credit and organized groups among farmers all

servative. During the election campaign of 1935, the Liberals promised reduced tariffs, a trade treaty with the United States, marketing reforms, new unemployment insurance, and securities control. This policy was less daring than Bennett's and coming from a reform party it was more credible. "King or Chaos" was a useful Liberal slogan that year.

In the election, Bennett and his party were soundly defeated and Mackenzie King and the Liberals formed the government with 173 seats. The Tories returned 40, Social Credit 17, and the C.C.F. 7. There were 7 "others." Mackenzie King took the New Deal legislation to the courts. The Judicial Committee of the Privy Council found most of it to be *ultra vires*, or beyond the authority of the federal Parliament, on grounds that it affected "the property and civil rights of the provinces." This was another example of the Privy Council's adopting an interpretation of the constitution unfavorable to a strong central government. Accordingly, it was a victory for "provincial rights." [12] It remained for King to implement much of the same legislation by the end of the decade once the necessary constitutional amendment was made.

As for the Conservatives, they disappeared as a major force for two decades. The party was discontented with its leader. Stevens, already mentioned as the leader of the Reconstruction Party, was but one member who objected to "Bennett of Tarsus," who has been described as a "monarch of the forest under whose shadow no sapling could reach full maturity." [13] Bennett had flirted with socialism and failed. Disenchanted with Canadian politics and tired, he resigned as party leader in 1938, sailed for England in the following year, became a British peer, and lived his remaining years near Guildford, Surrey. He left behind a party without the vitality, leadership, or organization to bring it back into office. A survivor of the Depression, when asked what he thought of Bennett, replied "We hated his guts." The hardships of the Depression years forced many people to think in similar terms.

12. F. R. Scott, "The Privy Council and Mr. Bennett's 'New Deal' Legislation," *Canadian Journal of Economics and Political Science*, III, No. 2 (May 1937), 234–41.

13. Ernest Watkins, "R. B. Bennett," *Conservative Concepts*, II (Spring 1960), 16. See also V. R. McLean, "Bennett of Tarsus," *Canadian Forum*, 15 (February 1935), 178–79.

When Mackenzie King came to power in October 1935, his large majority allowed him to reassume his natural stance of "wait and see." However, in keeping with general Liberal preference for freer relations with trading partners, his government signed, in that year, a treaty with the United States. This allowed for the reduction of American tariffs and the removal of some Canadian protectionist devices. Accordingly, American manufactured goods and Canadian staple products found better markets across the line. New agreements were made with Britain, and by 1938 Canada's position in the North Atlantic triangle was somewhat determined by the policies of Britain and the United States. Canada's tenuous position was described in the Report of the Royal (or Rowell-Sirois) Commission on Dominion-Provincial Relations, 1940, as follows:

> Canadian trade with both the United Kingdom and the United States is of a complementary nature, and is a classic example of a basically sound division of labour. While Canadian cereals feed Britain, British textiles clothe Canadians; while Canadian products of the forest and mine, processed by hydro-electric power, feed the industries of the United States, the coal and iron products of the United States equip Canadian factories.
>
> Canada's position is similar to that of a small man sitting in a big poker game. He must play for the full stakes, but with only a fraction of the capital resources of his two substantial opponents; if he wins, his profits in relation to his capital are very large, and if he loses, he may be cleaned out.

In domestic affairs, the Mackenzie King government sought a reappraisal of Canada's economic situation, especially of the inequalities of regional disparity. The Depression had made graphic the inability of provincial and municipal governments to deal with unemployment and relief. It had also indicated that the federal government should become the major force in social welfare. After investigating these matters, the Rowell-Sirois Commission recommended that the federal government be given exclusive powers of direct taxation in order that it could give adjustments grants to the provinces for the purpose of providing a national minimum in social services. It also recommended a federal responsibility for unemployment relief and insurance and social security. In an era of rising provincialism, however, Ontario, British Columbia, and Alberta rejected a scheme which seemingly would rewrite the B.N.A. Act. Nevertheless, a constitutional amendment of 1940 gave the federal government the right to establish unemployment insurance. Moreover, in the strain of war, it acquired the necessary taxation powers by signing agreements with each province. This dominance in taxation gave it the necessary preeminence to raise money for the war effort. Once again, local particularities had given way before the pressures of war, and Ottawa emerged triumphant in the field of taxation.

In Defense of Canada

While Depression lay like a blight across the land, the nation's stance to appeasement and rearmament reflected the desire of Canadians to live in a "fireproof house" far from the scorching flames of Europe. After the 1935 election, Mackenzie King reaffirmed his policy of no advance commitments, whether in relationship to the British Commonwealth or the United States. He fell back on the old rhetoric of when a crisis came "Parliament would decide." Canadian delegates to the League of Nations were warned in vague terms against making obligations. When, on November 2, 1935, Walter Riddell, the Canadian delegate at Geneva, implied that Canada would support the use of oil sanctions against Italy for her invasion of Ethiopia, the government publicly repudiated his action. There was some division in the country between those who supported collective security and those, especially in Quebec, who supported a position that the government should abandon sanctions altogether and certainly not take the initiative in the League of Nations in imposing sanctions against Italy. The government preferred to adopt a wait-and-see attitude in foreign affairs. Nor would it permit the Canadian defense department to cooperate with its British counterpart in planning and preparation for joint action in the event of war.

Though the government might have preferred a policy of noninvolvement, the course of events in Europe and Asia did not allow the Joint Staff Committee of the Department of National Defence to assume an ostrich posture. In 1936, that agency made an outline of Canada's defense problems. War with the United States was of little likelihood, and British policy of conciliation toward the United States meant that the risk of Canada becoming involved in an Anglo-American war was minimal. The rise of Japan was a different matter. Here the implications for Canada were clear: Canada could not secure her western coast without assistance from the British Commonwealth or the United States or perhaps both. As far as Europe was concerned, the impending outbreak in Central and Eastern Europe meant that ultimately Britain would be involved, and that Canada could not "remain unaffected by any development which holds an obvious threat to the continued existence, as a world power, of Great Britain. Should that danger appear in obvious form 1914 may be expected to repeat itself." The Joint Staff Committee was remarkably accurate in its predictions, and as Hitler moved into the Rhineland and brought about the Anschluss with Austria and the dismemberment of Czechoslovakia, the government came increasingly to the position that Hitler's designs would mean that Britain would eventually be embroiled in war.

But the government was slow to recognize the German menace. Hitler fascinated Mackenzie King, and the Berlin meeting of the two in June 1937 was productive of mutual understanding if nothing else. King supported Chamberlain and the British appeasers against Eden and Churchill, while J. W. Dafoe, editor of the *Winnipeg Free Press*, one of the few newspapermen who opposed appeasement in Canada, continued to warn "that between the fools and cowards in London and the madmen in Berlin the guns will go off." As late as March 30, 1939, the Canadian prime minister was holding to his line of noninvolvement and noncommitment. "The idea," he told the House of Commons, "that every twenty years this country should automatically and as a matter of course take part in a war overseas for democracy or self-determination of other small nations, that a country which has all it can do to run itself should feel called upon to save, periodically, a continent that cannot run itself, and to these ends risk the lives of its people, risk bankruptcy and political disunion, seems to many a nightmare and sheer madness." But on the very same day, Ernest Lapointe, the senior Quebec cabinet minister, was attacking the shortsightedness of Quebec in supporting neutrality. As he so well knew, national unity could not be preserved if Canada stood idly by when Britain was attacked.

Gradually, the leaders of English-speaking and French-speaking

Canada realized that they could not stand alone. Gradually also the filial, psychological, and democratic ties of the British Empire took on new meaning; the British affiliations that Mackenzie King and his followers had snubbed so long now became, for Canada, the *raison d'être* for war. Hitler's artfully contrived invasion of Poland brought a British declaration of war on September 3, 1939, and one week later Canada declared war on Germany. For the second time in a generation, Canada went to war to redress the imbalance of the Old World.

In 1939 as in 1914, Canada was prepared to contribute a large degree of manpower and material to the conflict. But the nation was not prepared for war. After 1918 the country's defense policy had been founded on a reluctance to make military preparations. The ideas of war and militarism repelled Canadians, and because they hoped for peace they thought it would endure. When war came, they were unprepared. No doubt French Canada and some members of the C.C.F. and other groups opposed to war hoped that Canadian boys would not have to fight overseas. They would have preferred an economic contribution to the war effort. Nonetheless, by 1945 the nation had been geared to total war, and at great cost to Canadian family life, the quality of life, and national unity. The nation's capacities in manpower, talent, economic production, and transportation were used to the full. Canada continued to grow as a world force, and her unique position between Great Britain and the United States meant that her relations with these two powers were remarkably close. Canada became, in Churchill's words, the "linch-pin" of the Anglo-American relationship.

The idea of total war was slow to take hold in Canada. A "limited liability" war, particularly during the "phony war," was popular in some camps. Mackenzie King could promise the nation that conscription would not be instituted, and this was welcome in Quebec. But it did not go far enough. In that province, Premier Duplessis called for a provincial election. "Quebec," he said, "will never be the creature of Ottawa. . . . A vote for Maurice Duplessis and his candidates will be a vote for our autonomy and against conscription. A vote against Maurice Duplessis or any of his candidates will be a vote for participation, assimilation and centralization." Lapointe considered this to be an act of national sabotage. However, he and other Quebec cabinet members had several cards to play: they proposed to resign if

Duplessis were reelected. Duplessis and Union Nationale were defeated; and the federal Liberals and the nation had won a great victory—a victory not for conscription but a victory against Quebec taking an unconstitutional stance against war. "Had the results gone the other way," Mackenzie King wrote, "Germany would have felt dismemberment of the British Empire had already commenced." In Ontario, as well, there was criticism of the federal government. Premier Mitch Hepburn pushed through a resolution attacking the government for not prosecuting the war in the way Canadians wished. Mackenzie King answered this threat by calling an election, and on March 26, 1940, his party was returned with a large majority.

Although Mackenzie King and the Liberals promised no conscription, it was nonetheless a matter of course that as the war proceeded and the Allied position deteriorated with the fall of France and the German invasion of Scandinavia in 1940, the government had to extend its emergency powers. The National Resources Mobilization Act of 1940 authorized the Governor-in-Council to make orders "requiring persons to place themselves, their services and their property at the disposal of His Majesty in the right of Canada, as may be deemed necessary or expedient for securing the public safety, the defence of Canada, the maintenance of public order, or the efficient prosecution of the war, or for maintaining supplies or services essential to the life of the community." It contained the important reservation that these regulations would not apply to the use of Canadian armed forces personnel outside of Canada. King had skillfully dodged the conscription issue. At the same time, he had instituted a state of total war as far as the country was concerned: and under the National Resources Mobilization Act, the government could control industrial and agricultural production, prices, and transportation, and persons could be drafted for home service only. It was a remarkable piece of legislation and quite representative of the government's determination to uphold national unity by defusing the conscription issue.

No one wanted to renew the anguish of the conscription crisis of 1917. But that legacy of the First World War became a subject of increasing public debate as the war progressed. Canadian losses in the early years of the war, except during the Dieppe landings in France in 1942, were not heavy. Canadian troops were not used in the North African campaign, but with the landings on Sicily and the invasion of Italy and the assault on northwest Europe, the Canadian Army was fully in action and in need of men. In April 1942, King had adroitly sought a release from his election promise of no conscription through a national referendum. The results, reflecting the racial division of the country, showed 64 percent of the population in favor of conscription and Quebec decidedly opposed. King had been released from his promise; his new policy became "not necessarily conscription but conscription if necessary."

By the autumn of 1944, however, the problem of having sufficient men in the Canadian armed forces to maintain strength could not be ignored by the government. Colonel J. L. Ralston, the Minister of Defence, insisted that conscription was necessary and submitted his resignation when the prime minister would not accept his advice. Mackenzie King, who recalled Lord Durham's famous words about "two nations warring in the bosom of a single state," could not reject the voice of English-speaking Canada for conscription.[14]

Moreover, the voluntary system did not work. In 1944 the conscription crisis ended with the government introducing conscription, a measure which allowed for 1600 home-service draftees to be sent overseas as replacements for casualties. No doubt this move saved the government from breaking up. Although Quebec was angered by these developments, and Quebec members of Parliament refused to support the government temporarily, French Canada knew that in the Liberals and Mackenzie King their interests were best served. He

14. In 1944, Ralston was in Europe and intended to return to Canada and to bring in conscription. Mackenzie King wrote in his diary the following telling words: "I could not bring myself to being the head of a government which would take that course—a course which might, after five years of war in Europe, and preparation for a year and a half of another war in the Pacific—lead to spurts of civil war in our own country. It would be a criminal thing, and would destroy the entire war record, as well as help to dismember the Empire, for I am certain that its after effects would be all in the direction of demand for complete independence, if not annexation with the U.S. Anything to be separated from being in wars because of Britain's connection with them. I want to see the Empire endure. It can only endure by there being complete national unity in Canada. This is going to be a trying experience for me" (C. P. Stacey, *Arms, Men and Governments: The War Policies of Canada, 1939–1945* [Ottawa: Queen's Printer, 1970], p. 443). King's remarks fully reveal the parameters of the conscription crisis.

had not chosen to use the forcing tactics of Borden in 1917; instead, by delay and indecisiveness he had let developments run their course, and this policy had been successful. As for the conscripts, many of them rioted in army camps such as Terrace, British Columbia, and disciplinary measures were taken against them. The legacy of the "zombies" (who would not serve overseas) cut deeply into the national psyche. The war had revealed just how divided the nation was between those who were willing to serve a larger cause by offering their lives if necessary and those who were determined to avoid national service overseas. This division represented at once the international and the isolationist desires of its people.

National unity had been preserved at great cost for the French and English in Canada. But what about the Japanese? For a nation that had championed the cause of minority rights it is a shocking fact that the government treated the Japanese in British Columbia so discreditably. Civil rights gave way before security. Even before Pearl Harbor, an inquiry had recommended that Japanese should not be brought into the military service and that they all should be registered with the police authorities and watched. In 1942, some 20,000 of them were moved to the interior of British Columbia and to the prairies, and of these, 76 percent were Canadian-born and another 15 percent were naturalized Canadians. Their fishing boats, houses, and properties were confiscated with little or no compensation. A further 4,000 were deported to Japan. The *Vancouver Daily Province* of February 28, 1942, in adapting Gray's *Elegy written in a Country Churchyard,* summed up the racist opinion of British Columbia and perhaps of the nation as follows:

> The curfew tolls the knell of parting day,
> The lowing Japs wind slowly out of sight,
> The refugee homeward plods his weary way,
> And leaves the world to darkness and to whites.

In the summer of 1945, after six long years, the war came to an abrupt conclusion, first in Europe and then in Asia. Some one million men and women had entered the Canadian armed forces, one-twelfth of the national population. The national industrial expansion through governmental controls had allowed Canada to produce $4 billion worth of materials for her allies. Both in staple products and manufacturing, the Canadian economy had worked to capacity. Shipbuilding and armaments manufacture, mining and agriculture were at peak levels. Railways and merchant marine were strained to the limit. In economic terms the nation worked hard for the Allied cause, while the Royal Canadian Navy provided convoy support for the ships that carried the men and materiel across the North Atlantic.

The war had important continental implications. The Hyde Park Declaration of April 1941 allowed for the United States to increase raw material purchases in Canada; at the same time Canadian imports from the United States, classified as British orders, were charged to the lend-lease agreement. Anglo-American defense arrangements had certain significance for Canada, and the United States acquired 99-year leases for bases at Newfoundland, the British West Indies, and Bermuda. Meanwhile, a joint Canadian-American board of defense had been established in keeping with the Ogdensburg Agreement of 1940, and new Arctic defenses and the Alaska Highway were built. The whole object was to establish continental defense. Canada cooperated with the United States for security reasons, and the forcing flame of war had an obvious penetrating influence on Canada. Continental defense that endured after 1945 made the quest for national identity that much more difficult.

No doubt the Second World War, like the First, made Canadians conscious of their own identity. Hugh MacLennan, in his *Watch That Ends the Night* (1959), wrote as follows of Canada coming of age:

> While the war thundered on, Canada unnoticed grew into a nation at last. This cautious country which had always done more than she had promised, had always endured in silence while others reaped the glory—now she became alive and to us within her excitingly so.

War had allowed Canadians to extend their interests to the wider world once more. Proud of their historical evolution within the British Empire-Commonwealth, they were also acutely aware of nationhood and making a living. Many would look on the past with pride, but most would recall the cleavages of Depression and the horrors of two world wars. These were experiences not easily forgotten in the uncertain years after 1945.

6

Dilemmas and Divisive Issues Since 1945

In the years since 1945 Canadians, like peoples of other nations and lands, have faced a number of dilemmas and divisive issues. These evolve around several themes which have enduring relevance in Canadian history: the ownership and occupation of land, the growth of cities, the fluctuations of foreign trade, the tensions in federal-provincial relations, and the shifts in international affairs. On reflection, the number of problems seems endless. Yet there are five main issues that have ongoing relevance to Canadians today. These are, first, America's economic impact; second, the simmering problem of Canadian-*Canadien* coexistence; third, growing regional identities and disparities; fourth, obstacles to cultural advancement; and last, Canada's role in world affairs. These domestic issues have been paramount and the search for Canadian separateness in the face of them so elusive or painful that Canadians have spent much time contemplating what they regard are their misfortunes as the "Scotland of North America." A glance at the developing world, however, should indicate to them that in terms of security, forms of government, standard of living, and freedom from want they are among the more fortunate inhabitants of the world.

Sleeping with an Elephant

Much recent Canadian self-reflection has focused on the theme of the so-called American economic "takeover." In the late eighteenth and early nineteenth century, Canadians had cause for alarm as two invading armies carrying American flags threatened Canadian soil. The Empire, however, provided British America with security and the attackers were repelled. Canada's Old World connection had given her a counterweight against American domination. However, as the nineteenth century advanced, American military and naval power continued to rise, an index of rapidly growing national economy and population. With the coming of Anglo-American rapprochement at the turn of the century, Canada no longer regarded Americans as a military threat. As the Prime Minister Wilfrid Laurier said in 1907, the defense of Canada lay in the Monroe Doctrine and the Royal Navy.

But, by the time of Laurier's remarks, another dominant strain was making itself felt on Canadian development. This was American investment. Sir John A. Macdonald had been conscious of keeping Canadian railway building in Canadian and British hands. Similarly, his national policy of 1879 was intended to build up the manufacturing capabilities of the Dominion. In reality, however, it encouraged American investment. American investors built branch plants behind the protective fence of the tariff. Soon some of the more prominent propagandists for the tariff were American members of the Canadian Manufacturing Association. Ironically, then, by 1911 the Conservative Party, backed by business interests, was fighting an election on the slogan "No Truck or Trade with the Yankees!" Certainly there is cause to believe that there was a great deal of truck and trade with the United States, and that the continental tendencies of resource exploitation, energy development, and international trade were already apparent.

This new American impact on Canada was a negation of previous Canadian economic development, which had been based in trade with Europe. As the great Canadian social scientist, Harold Innis, put it, Canada existed not in spite of geography but because of it. The development of her cod fisheries, fur trade, wheat farming, and forest industries gave unity to the theme of resource development.

For Innis, Canada's regions were not simply appendages of their American counterparts; the northern dominion had an east–west, transcontinental axis incorporating the water systems of the Atlantic, the St. Lawrence, the Great Lakes, the rivers of the West. And, perhaps more importantly, coupled with this was a transoceanic system linking Canada with Europe, especially with Britain and France, from which had come the demand, the political power, the military assistance, the ideas, the institutions, and the creative power that enabled Canada to maintain her identity and existence in the New World. For Innis and a whole school of economists and historians who were influenced by him, Canada and Europe were not mutually exclusive: the transatlantic links enabled Canada to offset the influence of American power, military as well as economic, on the North American continent.[1]

Today, Innis' remarks are highly relevant to an understanding of Canada's relationship to the American empire. We now realize that the old mercantilism of Europe has given way to the new mercantilism, the thrust of which is not only trade but also technology and corporate power, which have had by-products of industrialization and urbanization. The "old staples" of fur, fish, timber, and wheat have given way to the "new staples" of nickel, iron ore, oil, and natural gas. At the same time, the east–west axis that linked Canada to Europe has given way to the north–south axis that links Canada to the United States. This was brought about by the construction of the Panama Canal, by the rise of the port of Vancouver, British Columbia, and by the exhaustion of American mineral and timber resources, which was followed by the growth of similar resource exploitation in Canada.

Canadians since 1945 have spent much time agonizing over the long-range consequences of their "colonial economy." They acknowledge and by and large appreciate the part played by American enterprise and capital in building the country. However, they worry about the consequences of Americans having played that role so well. In some circles, particularly of the left, they fear that American influence will subvert Canadian sovereignty, and they demand that the first responsibility of their government must be to ensure that the national purposes—political, strategic, and economic—are achieved.

1. Harold Innis, "Great Britain, the United States and Canada," in his *Changing Concepts of Time* (Toronto, 1952), pp. 110–11 and 120–21.

Yet the paradox of Canadian desires for national self-determination is that the two countries share basic economic and political philosophies. They share in the processes of industrialization and urbanization. Growing economies, full employment, the free flow of capital are features of North American business capitalism; and it is because the two nations share this ideology that Canada has become a frontier of great American ownership.

Although the two countries are each other's best customer, it must be added that the much smaller country is prone to circumstances that the larger nation might not be aware of and is thus not sensitive thereunto. It is a common feeling among Canadians that Americans and the United States government do not always appreciate the unique slant of bilateral relations. Prime Minister Pierre Elliott Trudeau put it this way to a National Press Club audience in Washington in 1969: "Living next to you is in some ways like sleeping with an elephant. No matter how friendly and even-tempered is the beast, one is affected by every twitch and grunt."

Of all the twitches and grunts which most affect the mouse, the animal to which Canadians have likened themselves, the American business frontier in Canada has aroused the greatest response in Canada. Early in the twentieth century, Laurier remarked that "the twentieth century shall be the century of Canada and of Canadian development." By the middle of the century, it had become clear to some that Canada belonged to the United States in kind and degree.[2] In kind, American investment in Canada was not through the

2. On this subject, the reader's attention is directed to the following: Dave Godfrey with Mel Watkins, *Gordon to Watkins to You Documentary: The Battle for Control of Our Economy* (Toronto: New Press, 1970); Peter C. Dobell, *Canada's Search for New Roles; Foreign Policy in the Trudeau Era* (London: Oxford University Press, 1972); J. W. Warnock, *Partner to Behemoth: The Military Policy of a Satellite Canada* (Toronto: New Press, 1970); Stephen Clarkson, ed., *An Independent Foreign Policy for Canada?* (Toronto: McClelland and Stewart, 1968); Lewis Hertzman et al., *Alliances and Illusions* (Edmonton: Hartig, 1969); Kari Levitt, *Silent Surrender: The Multinational Corporation in Canada* (Toronto: Macmillan of Canada, 1970); Walter Gordon, *A Choice for Canada* (Toronto: McClelland and Stewart, 1966); Hugh G. J. Aitken, *American Capital and Canadian Resources* (Cambridge, Mass.: Harvard University Press, 1961) and, by the same author, *The American Impact on Canada* (Durham, N.C.: Duke University Press, 1959); James Laxer, *The Energy Poker Game: The Politics of the Continental Resources Deal* (Toronto: New Press, 1970); Melville H. Watkins, *Foreign Ownership and the Structure of Canadian Industry—Report of the Task Force* ("The Watkins Report") (Ottawa, Queen's

sale of bonds or debentures or noncontrolling equity stock, as had been the case during the nineteenth century when British capital built the country; it was through the influx of direct investment through branch plants and subsidiaries of parent companies in the United States. The difference in forms of investment is important: the former has the possibility of repaying the loan and ending the liability; the latter is a permanent liability with control probably remaining in the hands of the borrower. In terms of degree, the American penetration of the Canadian economy advanced rapidly after 1945. Direct investment in Canada grew from a book value of $2.4 billion in 1946 to $7.4 in 1956, to $13.9 in 1965, and to $21.1 in 1969. Presently over 80 percent of nonresident direct investment in Canada comes from the United States. By 1969 this had meant that U.S.-controlled corporations in Canada owned $35 billion out of a total value in corporate assets of $190 billion.

This growing American ownership has meant that control of certain key Canadian resources and industries passed into foreign hands. The resulting domination led the government to set up an agency to monitor foreign investment and control under terms of the Corporations and Labor Union Returns Act (CALURA). Its first report, in 1967, identified the following, with percentage control, as U.S.-owned: iron (85.8), oil and gas wells (65), fruit and vegetable canners (62.3), tobacco (16.8), rubber products (82.9), synthetic textiles (71.5), paper products (53.3), publishing (40.7), boiler and plate industries (68.9), metal stamping (60.3), hardware and tools industries (47.2), commercial refrigeration (59.4), aircraft industries (48.3), motor vehicles (95.6), truck bodies (55.8), small electrical appliances

---

Printer, 1968); A. E. Safarian, *Foreign Ownership of Canadian Industry* (Toronto: University of Toronto Press, 1966); John H. Redekop, ed., *The Star-Spangled Beaver* (Toronto: Peter Martin Associates, 1971); Al Purdy, ed., *The New Romans* (Edmonton: Hartig, 1968); Ian Lumsden, ed., *Close the 49th Parallel etc.: The Americanization of Canada* (Toronto: University of Toronto Press, 1970); Richard A. Preston, ed., *The Influence of the United States on Canadian Development: Eleven Case Studies* (Durham, N.C.: Duke University Press, 1972); and William H. Pope, *The Elephant and the Mouse: A Handbook on Regaining Control of Canada's Economy* (Toronto: McClelland and Stewart, 1971), pages 146–52 of which give a good bibliography of the subject and some indication of the voluminous nature of the periodical literature on the subject. A balanced treatment is given by John Fayerweather, *Foreign Investment in Canada* (Toronto: Oxford University Press, 1974).

(81.8), major appliances (58.5), industrial electrical equipment (89.6), battery manufacturers (73.6), petroleum refineries (72), fertilizers (49.7), pharmaceuticals (68.6), paints (67.1), soap (62.1), toilet preparations (66.4), industrial chemicals (58.9), scientific and professional equipment (62.0), and sporting goods and toys (51.3). The nonresident ownership figures, as distinct from U.S. foreign ownership, were slightly higher, showing nonresident ownership to be dominant in the following degree: mining industries 60 percent, metal industries 55.6, machinery industries 71.9, transport equipment industries 86.2, electrical products 65.7, petroleum and coal products 99.9, and chemical products 83.0. This lengthy catalog shows how American-controlled corporations dominate key resource and manufacturing industries.

A strong case could be made that even if the rate of U.S. investment in Canada were to diminish, as seems likely because of balance-of-payments difficulties in the United States, the growth of American operations north of the border would still advance. This can be supported by the fact that it is a distinct feature of the multinational corporation that capital investment comes mainly from profits made in the host country. According to the U.S. *Survey of Current Business* for January 1967, only 11.4 percent of the funds to U.S. subsidiaries comes in the form of a new capital inflow. Apparently Canadians, or the profits of American operations in Canada, finance the rest.

What impact does the financial power of Wall Street have on the producers and consumers of materials in the Canadian hinterland? A good deal. The new industrial system shows that the producer, not the consumer, dictates the choice of products and markets, and determines the technology, skills, and materials used. This phenomenon, variously described as "demonstration affect," "trickle-down effect," and "Cocacolonization," is part of the new mercantilism of the multinational corporation. The private corporate empires have penetrated the national economies, and the headquarters of these empires have the right to make the final decisions. Thus the Canadian complaint is with the multinational corporation—against General Dynamics, the Del Monte Corporation, General Foods (which makes Tang for Canadian taste but other products not necessarily for Canadian taste), or Quaker Oats. IBM, Gulf, Union Carbide, Ford, Proctor & Gamble, and General Tire are other examples of business empires with great influence on the Canadian economy.[3]

It goes without saying that if these corporations had head offices in Montreal, Toronto, Winnipeg, or Vancouver, Canadians might feel more comfortable. But New York, Chicago, and Los Angeles are the corporate centers of Canadian business. The technostructure (Galbraith's term) is south of the line. There, policies of production, design, research, engineering, and marketing are conducted and the possibilities of Canadian talent contributing to these various fields of business has diminished with the rise of the Canadian subsidiary and the multinational corporation and new stringencies in American immigration regulations.

No doubt these developments will make Canadian business less inventive, less venturesome. Canadians invented the telephone, the gas mask, frozen food, pablum, the electron microscope, and the automatic mail sorter. They also invented blind-landing systems for aircraft, the first automatically controlled machine tool, the variable pitch propeller, the electric organ, the paint roller, and the wire-photo transmitter. But manufacture of these inventions has been largely outside the country, particularly in the United States; and it is one of the telling features of Canadian invention history that Canadian businesses have been reluctant to back venturesome projects. Recent profiles of the takeover of Canadian business in Galt (now Cambridge), Ontario, as described in the interestingly titled book *Galt USA*,[4] are cases in point. Furthermore, 96 percent of all patents taken out in Canada in 1964 were by nonresident applicants, mainly American. A Canadian Royal Commission in 1960 reported Canada's growing dependence on foreign technology, an unhealthy sign for a nation which, because of the tyrannies of climate and distance, has had to be particularly inventive and resourceful.

During the late 1960s, the question of foreign ownership became the subject of increased governmental inquiry. Government measures for control of certain sectors of the economy were already established. For example, national control existed over the Bank of Canada, the Industrial Development Bank, Canadian National Railways, Air Canada, Telestat, Panarctic Oils, Canadian Overseas Communica-

3. Profiles of some of these companies may be found in Pope, *Elephant and the Mouse*, pp. 130–45.

4. *Galt, USA* (Toronto: Financial Post, 1971).

tions, Atomic Energy of Canada, and so on. And through agencies such as the Canadian Transport Commission, National Energy Board, and Canadian Radio-Television Commission, the government had regulatory powers. Foreign ownership was also controlled in banking, insurance, radio and television, and certain tax incentives, and tariffs existed to encourage Canadian production and prevent the domination of the Canadian market by imports.

But the private sector of the economy lay unprotected. Walter Gordon, an advocate of economic nationalism, resigned as Minister of Finance in the Pearson administration in 1968 when his colleagues refused to adopt his proposals for increasing Canadian ownership of the economy and his other suggestions for working in other ways toward national development. The Liberals did not advocate reform along corporate lines. But because of public pressure they appointed a commission in 1970 to investigate. The Gray Report, as it was named after its chairman, recommended a central agency to monitor all direct investment and thereby maximize the advantages and minimize the disadvantages of U.S. investment. The government did not adopt the Report as a blueprint for the "repatriation" of the Canadian economy. Instead, it first developed what amounts to a national mutual fund called the Canadian Development Corporation and second passed legislation—The Foreign Takeovers Review Act (1972) and The Foreign Investment Review Act (1973)—to screen foreign takeovers of Canadian businesses, regulate foreign investment with the cooperation of the provinces, impose license restrictions on transfers of technology into Canada, and require the majority of directors in federally incorporated companies to be Canadian citizens normally resident in Canada.

These policies were regarded by some as not going far enough. Walter Gordon and the Committee for an Independent Canada, the Waffle Group (a group of socialists that attempted, unsuccessfully, to radicalize the policies of the New Democratic Party), and the Canadian Labor Congress worked to advance Canadian ownership but did not do so in unison. Although Canadian governments may not be committed to nationalization of the economy on economic grounds, the pressures from the left, from labor, and from independent interest groups may be such that nationalization of certain industries may come for political reasons. The process is likely to be piecemeal and only when the need arises.

The most recent pressure on American interests in Canada is from Canadian labor. Of Canada's 2.2 million organized workers, three out of five union members pay their dues to U.S. "internationals" such as the United Mine Workers and the United Steelworkers. On an annual basis, this amounts to $40 million. Canadian workers complain that U.S. labor officials have far too much influence over Canadian wage contracts, that the United States internationals collect more in dues each year than they return in strike pay and other benefits, and that some dues money is being used in the United States to lobby for protectionist trade regulations such as the Burke-Hartle trade bill, which would place quotas on imports into the United States and cause the loss of 50,000 to 100,000 Canadian jobs. Accordingly, there has been a swing away from the U.S. internationals. In 1972 for instance, oil workers in Montreal and asbestos workers in the Yukon joined the Council of Canadian Unions; and in the same year, British Columbia aluminium workers deflected from the Steelworkers to join the Canadian Aluminium, Smelter and Allied Workers. On the basis of this it can be suggested that nationalism among union members may erode the influence of the international union movement in Canada in the future.

In all these aspects, Canadians are becoming increasingly aware of their economic dependency. They have also resisted a continental energy policy. This does not mean that they have been unwilling to sell natural gas, oil, electric power, coal, and nuclear energy to the United States. But it does mean that they want to sell it on their own terms—that is, on a normal commercial basis, not as a "continental energy deal."

In May 1971, Brice O'Brian, president of the U.S. National Coal Association, told a hearing of the U.S. Senate on energy resources that "our government considers Canada our own for energy purposes." How much this reflects American political and industrial opinion may be questioned, but in the following month, President Nixon said that one means of averting an energy crisis in the United States was to import vast quantities of Canadian energy, in the form of natural gas, oil, hydropower, and water. One senses, but cannot document very substantially, that recent United States official opinion classifies Canadian resources as continental resources, and that "common ownership" (a term of recent American origin) is a fact of life. Because U.S. sources of natural gas, coal, crude oil, hydropower, and water are either depleted or approaching depletion, and an "energy crisis" is at hand, the United States has little to share with Canada. But Canada has a lot to share with the United States. Any continental resources deal, Canadians realize, will mean that Canadian sources are part of a continental pool.

For the United States, the question of an adequate continental source of energy is tied to domestic needs and national security. United States national oil policy is to equate energy resources to military strategy and national security. As the oil resources of the United States diminish, pressures in government circles, more recently from Secretary of the Interior Rogers Morton and Senator Henry Jackson of Washington State, mount for a free exchange of energy resources and, to a lesser degree, for efficient means of transportation, by tanker and/or pipeline, of the oil and gas from the Alaska North Slope to the contiguous states. In 1970, the President's Task Force on Oil Import Control, chaired by George P. Schultz, a former Secretary of Labor, concluded its report, entitled *The Oil Import Question: A Report on the Relationship of Oil Imports to National Security*. It argued that in an emergency Canada might receive oil imports previously bound for the United States; that the reserve oil supply in Canada and the delivery system were inadequate for Canada and ought to be remedied by the Canadian government; and that until this situation had been corrected, the free flow of Canadian crude into the United States would be inadvisable. In other words, Canada ought to extend her means of domestic production and become more self-sufficient, and when these conditions had been met, the unimpeded entry of Canadian crude into the U.S. market would be allowed. It also recommended a continental energy deal with harmonious relations with Canada: mutual security and continental energy planning were to go hand in hand. And, as the report stressed, "the economic infrastructure of the United States is and can be far more integrated with that of Canada than with the economy of any other country in the western hemisphere." The Schultz committee did not stop with oil. It recommended that natural gas, coal, and hydroelectric and nuclear energy should be included.

During the 1950s, Canada engaged in a continentalist oil measure of her own. As early as 1931, a plan had been afoot to sell Alberta gas in Ontario, but it lay dormant until 1951, when Clarence Decatur

Howe, American-born wizard of the Canadian economy during World War II and Minister of Trade and Commerce, became interested. This "Minister of Everything," as the opposition liked to call him, was obsessed with the theory of getting things done. He was unconcerned with the giveaway of Canadian industry to foreign interests during the 1950s. Thus it mattered little to him whether a Trans-Canada pipeline was built with Canadian or American capital and control as long as it was built. The C.C.F. and the Conservatives disagreed.

Howe enjoyed his role of mediator between various interested promoters and petroleum companies. Shortly after the Korean War began, in 1950, when American supplies were uncertain, Howe proposed that natural gas from Alberta be transported to Vancouver and exported to needy American Pacific Northwest markets and war industries. He hoped to forestall Texas promoters, who were also planning a pipeline from the Southwest. Subsequently, Canadian authorities granted Frank McMahon and Westcoast Transmission the first gas export permit. However, only after McMahon made a deal with the Texas interests for joint marketing in the Pacific Northwest did the U.S. Federal Power Commission allow him to import gas into the United States. This continental energy deal in gas was eminently suitable to Howe, the petroleum interests, and to the U.S. government.

But Howe did not stop there. The Trans-Canada pipeline still had to be built, and without delay. In September 1955 he reached agreement with the provinces of Alberta and Ontario and Trans-Canada Pipe Lines, an American-Canadian company at face value but one actually controlled by U.S. capitalists. This pipeline would link Edmonton with Superior, Wisconsin, Chicago, Sarnia, Toronto, and Buffalo and half of its sales would be in the United States. The irony was that the Canadian government was to guarantee the project. Members of Parliament, the press, and the public wondered why the government should finance a company of *continental* rather than *Canadian* interests, and indeed, one controlled by American capital.

In the end, Howe and the Louis St. Laurent government had their way, but only after they resorted to closure to ram the legislation through Parliament in June 1956. The pipeline debate brought a debasement to the Canadian parliamentary process, and it showed the Liberals' commitment to the idea of a North American economy dominated by American capital. It also showed the Liberals' arrogance; and in the election of 1957 the Liberal era of twenty-two years came to an end and the Progressive Conservatives under John Diefenbaker were returned to power.

With regards to water, an American group calling itself the North American Water and Power Alliance proposed in 1966 the diversion of water from Canadian rivers into American deserts. The Canadian general A. G. L. McNaughton, a former Canadian chairman of the International Joint Commission, thought the scheme to be monstrous, and his theme was picked up and elaborated upon by the Canadian press. Why trade away Canadian water when Canadian needs for the future are unknown and the prospects for development to the direct benefit of the nation may be great? This argument has as its premise that Canada ought not to be just a resource base for United States industry, and that Canadians ought not just be hewers of wood, drawers of water, and players of hockey. And "the energy poker game," as James Laxer called it, has yet to be finished. But if it results in a continental resources deal it will define more fully than any previous development what Canada can or cannot do as a sovereign nation. It may signify the penultimate step toward annexation. Whatever the outcome, by 1970 it was clear that dealings were becoming more brittle, more obviously self-interested, and Canadians were aware of the challenges of sharing a continent with a vastly more powerful neighbor.

Such a momentous development as the voyage of the *S.S. Manhattan* in 1970, making feasible the commercial exploitation of the oil fields of the Alaskan Arctic by the Humble Oil Company, now an integral part of Exxon (which has its motto "A Country that runs on oil can't afford to run short"), brought distinct Canadian response. Prime Minister Trudeau's policy was sharp and firm: "Canada regards herself as responsible to all mankind for the peculiar ecological balance that now exists so precariously in the water, ice and land area of the Arctic archipelago." He also made clear that Canada would not permit a destruction of this balance "either in the name of freedom of the seas or in the interests of economic development." On the instructions of his government, Canadian sovereignty in the Arctic archipelago, inherited from Britain in 1880, was reasserted. Further, in the spring of 1970, the government extended the breadth of the territorial sea to 12 nautical miles, thereby closing the Northwest Passage. It also established a 100-mile pollution control zone in the Arctic and amended territorial fishing and shipping legislation to enforce pollution controls and fishing conservation measures. At about the same time, the U.S. Atomic Energy Commission's determination to proceed with exploding a five-megaton atomic device at Amchitka, Alaska, met with resistance from circles, official and unofficial, that had come to believe that the environment was worth preserving. No doubt the Canadian reaction also stemmed from Canada's firm support for the Strategic Arms Limitation Talks as well as reflecting the nation's skepticism of the United States' need to further demonstrate its nuclear superiority when risks to Canadian life and property were high. Finally, Canadian reaction reflected opposition to the Vietnam War and the Nixon surcharge.

Oil politics and nuclear testing are two features of the American empire that affect Canada greatly, and they are tied to Canadian strategic interests. The forcing flame of the 1939–1945 war intensified Canada's dependence on her neighbor for capital, equipment, and other imports. Continental defense arrangements in 1946, 1949, and 1958 brought, in turn, a joint agreement, NATO, and NORAD. Meanwhile, in keeping with the Hyde Park Declaration of 1941, Canada and her neighbor had developed programs for sharing defense production. Subsequently, a large armaments industry grew in Canada and under this arrangement, the United States procured in Canada, in the period 1959 to 1969, military items valued at $2,418.8 million. The corresponding Canadian defense procurement in the United States during the same period was $1,913.8 million. By 1969–1970, some 150 companies in Canada, employing 13,000 to 15,000 persons directly and 110,000 persons indirectly, were exporting about $300 million in defense equipment to the United States annually. In consequence, independence in Canadian foreign policy was somewhat compromised.

Clearly, war or preparation for war have become big business for the Canadian electronic and aircraft industry, but these economic benefits have obvious restrictions on Canadian foreign policy. Only from the New Democratic Party was criticism espoused that Canada ought to, like Sweden, stop all arms sales to the United States. But Sweden gave up annual arms sales amounting to only $1 million, and the economic consequences for a similar move on Canada's part would be great if not disastrous.

The agreement, nonetheless, has shown that continentalist tendencies can be promoted through defense-sharing arrangements and, at the same time for Canada, have revealed the dangers of free trade. Another cooperative manufacturing agreement, the Auto Pact of 1965, which provides unrestricted trade in automobiles and parts, has also assisted the growth of the Canadian economy. From 1963 to 1966, Canadian auto and auto parts exports increased from $37 to $841 million. That it has been so successful lies partly in the fact that the industry is, for all practical purposes, American-owned.

In future, such arrangements—in energy and manufacturing—will be conducted from the Canadian viewpoint of an *ad hoc* approach. Nonetheless, the arts of diplomacy may force Canada to, say, sell Peace River water to the American Southwest in order that the United States spend vast sums on environmental improvement and protection in the Great Lakes. In other words, it may be suggested that pressures from the metropolis may be exerted (or may continue to be exerted) on the hinterland; and in this connection the continuing energy and environmental crisis could result in Canadian-American relations being a subject of great moment.

In these circumstances, there is reason to believe that Canadian sovereignty is not in question. Although Canada is part of the American empire and the American impact on Canada has been extensive, Canada may well continue as a separate nation-state. Throughout history, informal imperial relationships have existed—with the British in Argentina, with the French in the Near East, and with the United States in Cuba after the revocation of the Platt Amendment in 1934. In none of these cases did annexation occur: the metropolitan power protected its own interests, mainly economic, without resorting to annexation. The principle of informal imperialism is probably at work in the Canadian context. Provided the American empire has access to the raw materials, energy resources, labor, and markets north of the border, Canadian sovereignty is assured. For Canada, independence in the classical sense of the nation-state may be impossible. The penetrating qualities of American business and culture—so representative of modernization and industrialization—will have a pronounced and continuing effect on Canada. We shall deal with the question of cultural dependency below.

The Not-So-Quiet Revolution

A second ongoing problem of modern Canada is its deep racial division at home. We have noted above that Canadians of French origin were incorporated as conquered people within British North America and that their leaders in clergy and politics realized that association with the English and the Empire was a counterweight to American republican institutions and a guardian of French-Canadian language, religion, and culture. But for many *Canadiens* the psychological effect of the conquest and of the rebellion of 1837 lay like a blight on the Quebec political landscape. Industrialism drew *Canadiens* to the cities, and many Quebec sons went to the thriving mill and factory towns of New England, where they married Protestant English-speaking women and abandoned their Quebec heritage of the land. English political and economic control, patronage, paternalism, and the divisiveness of war and conscription were not forgotten by those who remained behind. A character in Ringuet's great novel of the land, *Thirty Acres* (1938), put it this way: if the patriots of 1837 had won, the *Canadiens* "would be our own bosses and farmers' boys wouldn't have to go off to the States to make a living. . . . We wouldn't have the English sitting on our necks all the time and French-Canadians would stay good French-Canadians like in the old days." By 1930, when the Canada–United States ban on population interchange occured, some 1.1 million Franco-Americans had left for the United States, often taking with them the curse of the clergy and the anguish of family division.

In these circumstances, it is understandable that an urge for change or even revolution was emerging in Quebec. It was a development that certain *Canadiens* regarded as appropriate to the liberation movements in the Third World: they were colonial peoples seeking independence.[5]

The bombshell was dropped with the publication in 1961 of *Pourquoi je suis separatiste* by Marcel Chaput, a chemist and activist. "Since the end of the Second World War," he wrote, "more than thirty countries, formerly colonies, have been freed of foreign tutelage and have attained national and international sovereignty. In 1960

5. Cited in footnote 2, above.

alone seventeen African colonies, fourteen of them French-speaking, have obtained their independence. And now today it is the people of French Canada who are beginning to rouse, and they, too, will claim their place among free nations." Like other Quebecois desiring to speak for themselves, Chaput was saying that French-Canadians had no national thought of their own, that they did not control their own economy, that they were dominated by Anglo-Saxon North America, and that reforms were needed in Quebec to stop the French-Canadians from "smothering." His statement of national self-determination was based on four points: first, that French-Canadians form a nation; second, that the French-Canadian nation is a nation like any other; third, that Quebec is the rightful state of the French-Canadians; and fourth, if French-Canadians are to progress, they must be masters of their own house.

Chaput was not alone; "*maitres chez eux*" in Quebec and "*chez eux*" throughout Canada became appeals with which many French-Canadians could identify and with some reason. Political consciousness became a byword. In the National Assembly, the provincial legislature, a strong voice for sovereignty and independence was given by René Levesque, later to lead the *Parti Quebecois*. Outside the assembly, groups such as the *Rassemblement pour l'Independance Nationale*, the *Parti Republicain du Quebec*, and *Le Front de Liberation Quebecois* (F.L.Q.) and individuals such as Pierre Bourgault, André Larocque, Pierre Vallieres, and the leaders of the F.L.Q. proposed the remaking of Quebec in the socialist tradition—that is, making it a modern industrial state controlled and operated by and for the people who inhabit it. Although these groups might agree to the *ends* in view, they did not agree to the *means*. In fact they differed widely in their interpretations. Some, like Chaput, urged peaceful change; others advocated violent change.

What was called by some the "Quiet Revolution" of the 1960s had undercurrents of violence and instability. In February 1963 several bombings of public buildings and post boxes occurred and with loss of life. In that year the F.L.Q. issued its manifesto. "The separatist political parties," it pleaded, "will never gain sufficient power to overcome the colonizers' political and economic hold. Moreover, independence alone will not resolve anything. It must, *at all costs*, be accompanied by social revolution . . . QUEBEC PATRIOTS, TO ARMS! THE HOUR OF NATIONAL REVOLU-

TION HAS STRUCK! INDEPENDENCE OR DEATH!" By terrorist activity, the F.L.Q. was bent on a Marxist revolution in Quebec. The bombings and scares continued throughout the decade and reached a climax in the kidnapping of James Cross, a British Trade Commissioner, and the killing of Pierre Laporte, the Quebec minister of justice, in October 1970. The Quiet Revolution had entered a new phase.

The kidnapping and murder were a shock to the world and to Canadians who prided themselves, mistakenly perhaps, on the civil order of Canadian society. With anarchy at hand in Quebec, Ottawa acted on the recommendation of the provincial government. The government proclaimed a state of apprehended insurrection and issued regulations under the War Measures Act (1914) to preserve law and order by establishing a state of martial law and outlawing the F.L.Q. Although socialists both in and out of Quebec cried that this measure was a breach of liberty, the government held firm and Prime Minister Trudeau won the admiration of the nation for his courageous handling of the matter. Constitutionally, when "peace, order and good government" were threatened, the government had cause to act. As Lester Pearson said at the time, it is sometimes necessary for governments to take measures that seem to take away freedom in order to protect freedom. The arrest of the kidnappers and murderers brought a return to normalcy; as for the F.L.Q., it had been pushed underground but remained a possible threat to the state.

Meanwhile, events had occurred in Quebec and Ottawa that made the race question of even greater importance. In Quebec, modernization of education, nationalization of hydroelectricity, and limitation of the church's role in education occurred under the Lesage ministry as French-Canadians were becoming more aware of their social needs. On matters of taxation, Canada Pension Plan, and a proposed Medicare plan, Quebec demanded provincial control, and Ottawa agreed to an "opting out" formula whereby a province could receive the usual federal financial assistance in social services without being a partner in national schemes. Queen Elizabeth's visit to Quebec City in 1964 resulted in demonstrations and separatist reaction. DeGaulle's visit to Expo '67 and his famous statement, the cry of the separatists, "Vive le Quebec libre!" were unacceptable to the Canadian people and its government, Prime Minister Pearson informed the French president, and the latter cancelled his visit to Ottawa and returned dramatically to France. DeGaulle's remarks were in no way accidental; rather, they were the climax of Gaullist desire since 1960 to satisfy the need of French-Canadians for cultural support. They also came as a result of Quebec's deliberate moves to play a role in the French-speaking community, if necessary at the expense of Ottawa's central position in external affairs. In this process deGaulle had preferred to deal with ministers from Quebec City rather than Ottawa; federal ministers were ignored in Paris and the Canadian ambassador was snubbed. The Quebec-Ottawa disagreement over Quebec's aspirations for cultural and educational leadership in the francophobe Third World caused anglophobe disenchantment with Quebec.

Yet there was ample reason for complaint in Quebec. The "Quiet Revolution" was born of social and economic conditions, both urban and rural, that English-Canadians in similar circumstances would have found onerous. The French-Canadian in Quebec was dissatisfied with the power structure in his province, his inability to express himself outside Quebec, and his inability to direct his own destiny. Book III of the *Report* of the Royal Commission on Bilingualism and Biculturalism, published in 1969, recognized this condition: French-Canadians did not share equally with English-Canadians in socioeconomic levels, in upward mobility, in decision-making, in corporate ownership, in technology, in positions, in incomes, or in education. No doubt the Lesage legislation of the early 1960s aimed at rectifying this situation. But as the social revolution progressed so did the national revolution—socioeconomic advance and aspirations of the French-speaking sector went hand in hand, and in the Quebec elections of 1966, 1970, and 1973, "*la survivance*" was heard once more and the separatist vote climbed (in 1973 it was 23 percent). These developments augured poorly for building Canadian unity and self-confidence. Canada was at the crossroads: would it become one nation or two nations, or remain, as Lord Durham had observed in 1838, "two nations warring in the bosom of a single state"?

This question was in part answered by the Liberal victory in the 1968 federal election. The impact of Prime Minister Pierre Elliott Trudeau on the great national question was substantial. Born in Montreal in 1921, Trudeau was raised in a bilingual, bicultural family. After an excellent private education, he studied law, economics, and political science at Montreal, Harvard, Paris, and London. His return to Canada in 1949 coincided with his desire to attack the marriage of Church, business, rural society, and right-wing nationalists in Quebec. He and his friends sought to expose the corruption, deceit, immorality, and facade of Maurice Duplessis and *Union Nationale* and the ignorance perpetuated by the Roman Catholic church and its education system. Through their magazine *Cité Libre* they attacked conservatism as unprogressive. Social and economic thought in Quebec, they stated, had not kept pace with urbanization and industrialization; and the persons to blame were the politicians, educators, nationalists, and ecclesiastics. In 1956 Trudeau organized the *Rassemblement*, which called for a broadened left in Quebec, and in 1960 he helped the Liberals defeat the Union Nationale in the provincial election. This so-called "Quiet Revolution" of the 1950s transformed Quebec, and Trudeau wrote of this in *Cité Libre* as follows:

> . . . around 1960 it seemed that freedom was going to triumph in the end. From 1945 on, a series of events and movements had combined to relegate the traditional concepts of authority in Quebec to the scrap-heap; the post-war stirrings, "Refus Global," Asbestos, the unions, the judicial victories of Frank Scott and of Jacques Perrault, *Cité Libre*, the defeat of the Union Nationale, just to give some diverse examples. So much so that the generation entering its twenties in 1960 was the first in our history to receive fairly complete freedom as its lot. The dogmatism of Church and State, of tradition, of the nation, had been defeated. Authority had returned to its proper place in a free system. A lawyer could head the Lay Movement without losing his clients. Professors could say "no to the Jesuits" without being barred from the university. Comedians and movie producers could subscribe to Marxism without being discharged from the government corporations. Students could try to impose their views on educational institutions without being kicked out. The Family itself had lost its power over young men and young women.

In 1960, everything was becoming possible in Quebec, even revolution.[6]

6. The most popular if factually inaccurate and Marxist view of this was Léandre Bergeron's *The History of Québec: A Patriot's Handbook* (Toronto: New Canada Press, 1971), translated from the original *Petit manuel d'histoire du Québec* (Montréal: Editions Québécoises, 1970).

However, Trudeau soon objected to Jean Lesage and the Quebec Liberals' desire to reduce federal powers to nothing. Accordingly, he entered politics as a member of the federal Liberal party in order to defend federalism. In 1968, after only three years in the party, two years as a member of Parliament and one as Minister of Justice, he became leader of the party and prime minister. At age 47 he was a relatively young man for the office.

Trudeau's policies reflected his longstanding views on nationalism and race. He rejected the idea of "separate status" for Quebec, and instead argued that federalism necessitated counterweights. In this connection, he said that the British North America Act was a favorable device for *Canadiens* to fulfill their destiny and their economic, social, and cultural goals: it gave provinces jurisdiction over local matters—including education, property, and civil rights—and social and labor legislation, and only restricted Quebec on divorce and broadcasting. Thus Trudeau reasoned that Quebec had no need to evolve into a nation-state or even have special status in the nation. The corollary of his argument is that the rise of Quebec as a nation-state would end federalism and place Quebec in a position as a minority state. Trudeau urged the French-Canadians not to retreat into their own nationalistic shell but instead to abandon their ghetto mentality and enter boldly into the Canadian experiment, becoming in the process equally at home in Ottawa and Quebec. As for English-Canadians, he warned that they must accept the French presence, and not look on the nation-state as an Anglo-Saxon creation. The protection and realization of their ethnic qualities and aspirations should be done within a regional framework, not a pan-Canadian one.[7]

Trudeau's sophisticated arguments were among the most serious attempts to formulate a political theory for Quebec and Canada in the postwar period. Certainly they were a great counterweight to separatism. Yet Trudeau in practice was not as convincing as Trudeau in theory. He brought French-Canadians to the seats of power in Ottawa; he introduced regulations for making the civil service and army officer corps bilingual; and he promoted the dialogue between the French- and English-speaking peoples through student exchange schemes. Above all, he introduced legislation, the Official Languages

7. Pierre Elliott Trudeau, *Federalism and the French Canadians* (Toronto: Macmillan of Canada, 1968), pp. 65, 66–67, 206.

Act, that made French and English official languages of Canada in federal government administration. But bilingualism, as Trudeau was to find, could not be legislated, and the existence of an overabundance of inexperienced and incompetent French-speaking cabinet members as well as the seemingly undue preferences given French or bilingual persons in Ottawa brought on what has been called the English-speaking backlash of the 1972 election, in which the Liberal majority of 1968 was reduced to a minority at Ottawa. Though bilingualism and biculturalism had been adopted as government policy, on the basis of the report of a royal commission on the subject, the process of cooperative federalism continued to be painful and exasperating. However, had it not always been so? Had not each, as Trudeau knew, the power to break the country?[8] And as Canada entered the last quarter of the twentieth century the problems of federalism meant that the house was divided by languages if not by cultures.

Growing Regional Identities and Disparities

We have noted above that there has been a move in Quebec for a French-speaking society with its own distinctiveness. This has constituted a pragmatic protest against lack of economic opportunity and political control. It reflects Quebec's desire to bring itself into a technologically and industrially advanced urban society structured along the lines of French language and cultural expectations. The objective is identity and economic development. This is one of the types of regionalism and disparity that has emerged within Canadian federalism since 1945.

Since 1945 Canada has experienced two types of federalism. First, there was cooperative federalism, in which the provincial and federal governments no longer operated in unison as during the two world wars or in isolation as during the Laurier years and the interwar period. The governments engaged in cooperative ventures. Activities were coordinated and responsibilities were delegated, especially the spending of federal monies by provinces and municipalities in such things as university, college, and technical education, social welfare, and public works. The provinces had been brought within the dictates

8. "In terms of *realpolitik*, French and English are equal in Canada because each of these linguistic groups has the power to break the country. And this power cannot yet be claimed by the Iroquois, the Eskimos, or the Ukranians." *Ibid.*, p. 31.

of a nationwide and interdependent economy with nationwide interests and outlook. In these circumstances, Ottawa assumed or took responsibility for guiding the national economy and taxation policy. In 1947 Ottawa arranged a tax-rental agreement with all provinces except Ontario and Quebec by which the provinces rented their rights in income and succession duties tax fields to the Dominion. Though Ontario was later included within this scheme, as was Newfoundland, which became Canada's tenth province in 1949, Ottawa relaxed its adamant position with respect to Quebec, which wanted (and in the end kept) direct provincial taxation control to avoid anything that appeared to be double taxation or federal invasion of provincial rights.

By the mid-1950s, the provinces had become acutely aware of the need for economic growth. They wanted the exploitation of natural resources to fall completely within their realm. They also wanted funds to provide social security for the old, infirm, disabled, destitute, unemployed, and the like. Finally, they wanted monies to spend on city and intercity transportation, education, housing, and airports. An urbanized population required new strategies for spending money and conducting federalism. The change came in 1957 when Prime Minister Louis St. Laurent's government dealt with the latter need in a series of five-year tax agreements with the provinces. This gave the provinces more freedom to spend federal monies. Part of income tax and all of succession duties became provincial responsibilities. In addition, unconditional equalization grants became available to all provinces to bring their per capita tax incomes up to those of the two highest provinces.

The result of this swing from federal to provincial initiatives in fiscal policies has been called "double-image federalism," which includes "both the straightforward central-regional relationship between the central and provincial organs and a special relationship between French and English which to some extent transcends the other."[9] In this scheme of things Quebec took a hard line. As Premier Daniel Johnson said at a federal-provincial tax structure meeting in 1966, there exists in Canada a nation that speaks French, whose home is Quebec, and that needs the instruments for its development. "As the mainstay of a nation," he spoke of Quebec, "it wants free rein

9. J. R. Mallory, "The Five Faces of Federalism," in P. A. Crépeau and C. B. Macpherson, eds., *The Future of Canadian Federalism* (Toronto: University of Toronto Press, 1965), p. 3.

to make its own decisions affecting the growth of its citizens as human beings (i.e., education, social security, and health in all respects), their economic development (i.e., the forging of any economic and financial tool deemed necessary), their cultural fulfilment (which takes in not only arts and literature, but the French language as well), and the presence abroad of the Quebec community (i.e., relations with certain countries and international organizations)." The last point warrants underlining, for Quebec had by then developed extensive relations with the French-speaking world in Africa and elsewhere and even supports French language instruction of persons of Acadian or Canadian heritage in Louisiana.

Ottawa, during the premierships of Lester Pearson and Trudeau, was not willing to accept this type of federalism. To these leaders it would have led to a federation of two national collectives: one, French-speaking, dividing loyalties between Canada and Quebec; the other, English-speaking, owing its loyalties to a single Canadian state. This issue remains unresolved because Quebec's demands for virtually a separate status or a two-Canada concept collides with other provinces' and indeed the federal government's view that the Canadian nationality includes peoples of many cultures, races, and languages who owe common allegiance to one sovereignty. There can be no doubt that the estrangement of French and English one from another has provided a major obstacle to the development of Canada as an entity.

Other provinces have exerted demanding positions. Unlike Quebec, however, their emphasis has not been compounded by cultural questions but is instead based on regional economic disparity, resource control, or the drive to have increasing direction over monetary spending. Urbanization has affected each province, though some more so than others. Whereas the urban population of Canada was 56 percent in 1945 (in 1851 it had been 13 percent), by 1973 it approximated 80 percent. Ontario, Quebec, and British Columbia have experienced urbanization to a greater degree than the other provinces. Similarly, their metropolitan cores—Toronto, Montreal, and Vancouver—have outdistanced rivals within those regions.

As has been mentioned before, the transformation of Canada from a rural to an urban society has brought many problems. The urban environment with its crime, poverty, pollution, and transportation needs has placed new challenges on authority, and the quality of life in Canada and the expectations of its inhabitants is being transformed by this phenomenon. Canadian federalism, as noted above, has changed to reflect these facts.

What has happened to the rural areas, to the villages and small towns, the farms and ranches? The vast area of Canada remains productive in spite of urbanization. Saskatchewan's wheat industry, for instance, is now run by a more collectively organized industry with higher yields than before. Elsewhere, ghost towns and abandoned farms remain as testaments to another, less technologically advanced and industrial society.

In the face of these changes, provincial governments and regions have vied for more of the federal dollar. Let us deal with these in turn, from west to east. British Columbia's population and economy has grown steadily since 1945, and its populace has a relatively homogeneous outlook somewhat like Ontario. Though there is little discontent at the provincial level, and though the introduction of N.D.P. government came in 1972 and led to a reexamination of policies, what discontent there is is against the federal government. Education, welfare, and resource management have developed as highly prized provincial responsibilities. Financially strong and appropriately situated on the Pacific rim to take advantage of trade with Canada's second largest trading partner, Japan, British Columbia has profited much from east–west Canadian trade. Because of its suspicion of many federal policies, the British Columbia government, led by W. A. C. ("Wacky") Bennett, took an independent position in natural resources development, and, on the province's insistence, Canada signed the Columbia River Treaty with the United States in 1962. This allowed for a continentalist development of the Columbia River watershed which crosses the 49th parallel. The legacies of this decision, which include destruction of wilderness and recreation areas, financial loss and indebtedness, and Canadian-American tension over raising flood levels of dams for increasing hydropower potential, are among the most contentious issues in British Columbia politics. Talk of secession from the Canadian union has received more press than it deserves: British Columbia is a strong province within the confederation and its people continue to look for the full benefits of the union, a not altogether uncommon fact in Ontario or Quebec.

The prairie provinces—Alberta, Saskatchewan and Manitoba—have also looked for maximum benefits from confederation. Each has sought and in some cases gained from federal policies designed to market grains abroad. Traditionally, Prairie persons have regarded the national tariff with its high costs of transportation and eastern industrial commodities as economic colonialism. Producing 60 percent of Canada's agricultural yield, the Prairies believe that industrial interests in Toronto and federal interests in Ottawa do not provide appropriate reciprocal benefits. Cooperatives, socialism, and collectivist political parties have emerged from this regional discontent. On the other hand, the federal-provincial tax arrangements and the allocation of resource royalty revenue to the provinces have meant that the three capitals—Edmonton, Regina, and Winnipeg—have individual perspectives. But the anti-Ottawa stance is strong, a fact underlined by the energy "crisis" of 1973–1974 when oil was never in short supply in Canada (and export levels to United States markets were maintained) while Alberta, Saskatchewan, Ontario, and Ottawa argued about profits, royalties, and costs to consumers.

On the endless acres of Prairie landscape a unique perspective evolves among the occupants of city and farm. Physical isolation, physical unity through climate and prairieland, and sectional discontent continue to be central to the Prairie West's identity. But until confederation, which was designed to increase the wealth of central Canada, is changed, injustice, myth, and ideology will be fundamental to that region's consciousness.

The Prairie provinces are separated from Ontario by the upper Great Lakes—vast bodies of water—and fringed on the north by the rocky Canadian Shield. The psychological distance between Winnipeg and Toronto is immense. Ontario has its own regionalism. It is founded in industrial and agricultural development in the heavily populated area called southern Ontario, between Windsor and Kingston. Here one-third of Canada's population lives, and here also are the capital, entrepreneurial skills, and industries which Prairie, Quebec, and Maritime interests alike regard as the moguls of the nation. Closely tied to the United States industrial heartland and centrally located on the national east–west axis, yet blocked from eastern Canada by French culture and from western Canada by the tyrannies of distance, Ontario regionalism has a strong identification with the urban metropolis at Toronto, the abundant agricultural areas of southern Ontario, and to a lesser degree the "escape valve" of northern Ontario's lakes and forests. Ontario's parochialism is countered in some circles by a pan-Canadianism, a national identification in which Ontario is central to the past, present, and future of the nation.

The Maritimes also have a strong regional identity, but it would be a mistake to assume that Newfoundland, Prince Edward Island, New Brunswick, and Nova Scotia have similar societies, politics, and identities. Each is unique. Yet in relation to both Ottawa and central Canada as a whole their similarities are well-defined. The crux of the problem is economic. As the nineteenth century closed, the era of wood, wind, and water came to an end, and by the 1920s the "Maritime Rights" movement demanded (and got in 1926) a reduction in freight rates to Central Canada. The movement agitated for closer ties with the United States and countries overseas for the purposes of trade. One federal government response was to pass legislation in 1935 to subsidize the transportation of Maritime area coal. In 1939 various relief, unemployment, and emergency payments were granted to the provinces. In 1957 the Gordon commission recommended the moving of surplus populations to more productive areas. Generally, population and productivity declined in spite of diversity; federal attempts to provide solutions for maintaining viable provincial economies did not seem to work, and a well-known saying has emerged: "The more things change in the Maritimes the more they remain the same."

Beneath the rhetoric of Maritime discontent lies political manipulation of the frustrations of ordinary fishermen, farmers, and workers by the economic, social, and political establishment against Ottawa rather than against provincial capitals.[10] By projecting their inabilities on the "Upper Canadians" and by demanding more federal monies, the Maritimes have become increasingly incapable of self-sufficiency. And the paranoid style of their politics is well known across the country. They have been among the strongest beneficiaries of the trend since 1969 toward regional economic expansion under federal government monies, the purpose of which is to ensure that economic growth will occur in regions where growth and employment opportunities lag behind the normal rate of national economic growth.

10. G. A. Rawlyk, "Nova Scotia Regional Protest, 1867–1967," *Queen's Quarterly*, LXXV (Spring 1968), pp. 105–23.

Canadian Culture

The history of man living in Canada, both before the coming of the Europeans and since, is a record of survival: life for Canadians has been a "bread and butter" matter. The focus on survival has often meant adaptability to climate and terrain. It has also meant invention—invention to overcome the tyrannies of time and distance, hardship and cost, pain and loneliness. Accordingly, the technical achievements of Canadians, past and present—the canoe, whether birch bark or cedar, the Red River cart, the York boat, the telephone, and radio devices for locating downed aircraft, for instance—reflect these themes of Canadian life. In the arts and letters, architecture and engineering, crafts and inventions, the same features of survival and adaptability appear.

This tells us a good deal about the Canadian heritage. It suggests, for instance, why Canadians of European extraction have an obsession with failure, peril, and death, why they buy more insurance per capita than any other nationality, and why they have developed a welfare state in advance of their American counterparts. It suggests also why they are so concerned with who they are and whether their nation is a healthy body or a lively corpse or, in fact, whether Canada is a nation at all. Introspection has become a national pastime. Perhaps in George Grant's *Lament for a Nation*, published in 1965, this obsession reached its zenith.

By contrast, this suggests that American life may be dominated by the will to win and live. Where Canadians might adapt to harsher geographical circumstances, Americans might control and consume a less rigorous landscape.

The theme of survival in northern latitudes permeates Canadian culture. It was and is to be found in certain Indian and Eskimo artistic traditions. Whether in Newfoundland, Quebec, Saskatchewan, or British Columbia, the Canadian cultural accent is the same. Regional differences provide variety to the artistic scene, and the majesty, danger, and loneliness of the northern landscape are revealed in the paintings of Tom Thomson, A. Y. Jackson, Arthur Lismer and other members of the "Group of Seven." The same landscape has provided inspiration for writers. Louis Hémon's *Maria Chapdelaine* (1916), Susanna Moodie's *Roughing it in the Bush* (1852), and Ralph Connor's *Man from Glengarry* (1901) show how terrain and climate have dictated a hard life—one of struggle, toil, hazard, action, sensibility, and especially when Hémon called "the rough battle with the soil." The Canadian landscape with its distinctive seasons, so heartily appreciated by John Kenneth Galbraith in his *The Scotch* (1964), was well appreciated by Hémon, who wrote of "the marvel of the reappearing earth in springtime, after the long months of winter." The impact of geography is also apparent in the architecture of Erickson and Massey, the poetry of Robert Service and Earle Birney, the novels of W. O. Mitchell and Eric Collier, and the music of Violet Archer and John Beckwith. Often the results are harsh, bold, stark, painful, even ugly. But for Canadians in search of an identity it is Canadian.

If the features of Canadian culture have been fashioned mainly by the harshness of the land and climate, it is also certain that the thrusting influence of the United States has played a role in modifying European traditions transplanted to Canada. Since 1945 especially, North American attitudes toward business, aesthetics, media, race, and politics have prevailed. The interplay has produced a curious mixture, according to one observer: "We've had access to American know-how, British political wisdom, and French culture. Somehow we've managed to end up with British know-how, French political wisdom and American culture."

Concern for the future of Canadian culture was extensive in the late 1940s. There existed a real fear that the Canadian identity, such as it was, was being consumed by monolithic American influences. The resulting inquiry—the Royal Commission on National Development in the Arts, Letters and Sciences—reported in 1951 that United States influence was dominant in Canada and stood as the main obstacle in the way of Canadian cultural advancement. Named after its chairman, Vincent Massey, a Canadian statesman and governor-general, the Massey Commission announced a cultural principle of "Canada First": "That it is desirable that the Canadian people should know as much as possible about their country, its history and traditions; and about their national life and common achievements; that it is in the national interest to give encouragement to institutions which express national feeling, promote common understanding and add to the variety and richness of Canadian life, rural as well as urban."

The Commission's report, surely one of the great state papers in Canadian history, recommended the maintenance and extension of the Canadian Broadcasting Commission, the National Film Board, the National Gallery, the National Museum, and the Public Archives of Canada. A National Library and a Museum of Canadian History were recommended, but only the library has been built. The Commission also recommended support for persons in the arts and letters, broadcasting, film, and the press, either in or out of Canada. A bureau was to be set up to implement these suggestions, and in 1957 the Canada Council, endowed with $100 million, came into being.

The report also suggested that the federal government make annual contributions to advanced education, both university and technical. The Commission recognized the importance of universities as local centers of education, patrons of culture, and servants of the national cause. It recommended that these "nurseries of a truly Canadian civilization and culture" should be adequately financed through federal support.

After 1945 the growth of the Canadian university community reflected the growing interest of the Canada Council, the federal government, and provincial governments in education. Ontario, which had seven degree-granting institutions in 1867, built ten new universities after 1945, and assisted church-affiliated institutions. Quebec, British Columbia, and Alberta developed rigorous programs of expansion and other provinces followed suit. As of 1971, Canada had sixty-six degree-granting institutions, a ratio of one university for every third of a million people. From 1945 to 1969 the Canadian university student body grew from 52,500 to about 300,000, and this came in response to the "baby boom," the Sputnik era, and public demand for university education.

However, a comparison with the United States reveals that in 1960 9.2 percent of the 20- to 24-year-old group enrolled in institutions of higher learning in Canada, whereas 30.2 percent enrolled in the United States.[11] Although this may tell us as much about American as Canadian society, it seems undeniable that a Canadian univer-

11. Seymour Martin Lipset, *Revolution and Counterrevolution*, rev. ed. (New York: Anchor Books, 1970), pp. 40–43. Lipset's analysis of Canadian education as showing a more elitist society north of the line is suggestive and interesting but not conclusive.

sity education was not available to Canadians to the same degree as its counterpart was to American youth. This was particularly noticeable in graduate studies. Canadian universities neglected advanced studies, and Canadian scholars were not being trained at home. Instead, they went to Oxford and London, Harvard and Berkeley. With the expansion of Canadian universities in the 1960s it was natural in the circumstances that Canada grew reliant on outside academic help. In 1968, for example, 86 percent of new faculty appointments went to non-Canadians, especially Americans. In 1969–1970 the citizenship of Canadian university faculties was 58.7 percent Canadian, 16.2 percent American, 10.1 percent British, 2.1 percent French, and 12.9 percent from other countries. The percentage of Americans (16.2) stood in contrast to the 2.5 percent of the faculty of American universities who were not U.S. citizens and the 3 percent in Britain who were not British subjects. Canadian universities had allowed a situation to develop which Hugh MacLennan, the novelist, thought had amounted to "a program of national suicide."[12] The so-called Americanization of Canadian universities became a matter of public concern in the late 1960s and 1970s, and the fear was that if the trend continued it would change significantly the texture of Canadian higher education, particularly in the arts and letters, social sciences, and humanities—those areas of academic endeavor recognized by the Massey Commission as contributing most to the quality of national life and culture. Meanwhile universities were becoming increasingly bureaucratized, and instead of being creative institutions of society increasingly took on the guise of creatures of provincial ministries of education.[13]

In mass media, also, Canadian culture was under attack. *Time* and *Reader's Digest*, the major periodicals sold in Canada, were American-owned but contained little Canadian content, and they

12. Quoted in Robin Mathews and James Steele, *The Struggle for Canadian Universities: A Dossier* (Toronto: New Press, 1969), p. 1. For statistical data on foreign appointments, see *University Affairs/affaires universitaires*, September 1970, p. 4.

13. Ironically, federal monies had contributed greatly to the building of these institutions for the purpose of developing *Canadian universities*, not *provincial institutions*. Quebec's zealous guarding of provincial rights in education, however, destroyed the broader federal concept; and after 1966 federal grants went not directly to the universities through the Association of Universities and Colleges of Canada but directly to the provinces.

were excluded from taxes imposed on foreign periodicals sold in Canada. Canadian national publications such as *MacLeans* and *Saturday Night* continued to operate, while *Canadian Forum* and *Canadian Dimension,* both oriented toward the left, told of the plight of Americanization. Book publishers like Ryerson and W. J. Gage fell to foreign control; and the majority of university and library bookstore purchases were books not published or printed in Canada. By the mid-1970s the federal government and Ontario had developed funds for assisting Canadian-owned publishers.

Meanwhile, the Canadian Radio and Television Commission recommended percentages of "Canadian Content" on C.B.C. programming against the purchase of non-Canadian manufactured textbooks. But somehow, Hollywood, "Sesame Street," *Time,* and the World Series had become part of Canadian life and Canadian children could cheer as easily for the Boston Bruins, New York Rangers, or Philadelphia Flyers as they could for the Montreal Canadiens, Toronto Maple Leafs, or Vancouver Canucks. After all, the teams were almost Canadian to a man. Canadians, through advances in communications, had become part of a North American culture, and what the Toronto-based Marshall McLuhan called "the global village" was a concept well understood by Canadians.

Canada and the Wider World

Since 1776, Canada's position in the wider world has been tied up with two political entities. One is the British Empire; the other is the United States. And the relationship between these two has sometimes benefited Canada and sometimes not. Canada sought to survive in North America in immediate proximity to a nation which through the course of two centuries was developing into the most productive, most militarily capable power yet seen. She had often looked to the United Kingdom and the British Empire as a counterbalance to United States' influence. However, by 1945 it was clear that the prevalent factor in Canada's relationship was not the British Commonwealth, in which she had played such a part in its evolution into a group of autonomous, self-governing dominions. Instead it was the United States that became the principal determinant in the Canadian existence. And in this shift of metropoles the search for a Canadian identity became increasingly difficult. Rejecting opportunities afforded by the Commonwealth for her own leadership, she withdrew again to the continental heartland.

The economic development and continental pull of the postwar period brought Canada closer to the United States, as we have seen. That relationship was also strengthened by the similarities in the foreign policies of the two North American powers. This association of powers was slow to emerge. Canada worked toward developing a strong British Commonwealth, not of the centralized variety as proposed by Lionel Curtis at the 1945 Commonwealth Relations Conference in London, but of the loose type advocated by the Canadian nationalist E. J. Tarr. Canadian policy was that world stability could best be achieved by strong yet associated countries within the Commonwealth, and the Liberals pursued this policy in the postwar period. Canada worked toward admitting India, Pakistan, Ceylon, Ghana, Nigeria, and other nations into the new multiracial Commonwealth, some of them as republics. Her pressures for reducing racism in South Africa led to that nation withdrawing its application for membership in the Commonwealth.

Another preoccupation with the government was the objection to independent initiatives in foreign affairs. No doubt this represented the opinion of Mackenzie King, the prime minister until 1947. His Liberal successors, St. Laurent and Pearson, adopted modifications of his point of view. In 1946 St. Laurent became Secretary of State for External Affairs, a move which Mackenzie King judged would reassure French-Canadians that they need not fear an "internationalist" foreign policy. Canada was in no position, St. Laurent said in 1947, to assume a position of leadership in world affairs: "There is little point in a country of our stature recommending international action, if those who must carry the burden of whatever action is taken are not in sympathy." Although King had little faith in supernational organizations, Canada became a founding member of the United Nations in 1945, took part in all the UN agencies, and in 1950 joined the Columbo Plan for economic and technical assistance in overpopulated and underdeveloped world areas. In doing this, the nation agreed to the general purposes of the new bodies—that is, the maintenance of international peace and security, development of friendly relations between states, and achievement of cooperation in solving international economic, social, cultural, and humanitarian problems.

Nonetheless, the course of world affairs, especially the development of the Cold War, brought Canada out of isolation. With the sensational Gouzenko revelations of 1945–1956, the nation became aware of a Soviet spy ring in Canada. The Truman Doctrine of 1947 placed Canada among a group supposedly antagonistic to the life of the communist states. The workings of the Joint Board of Defence brought the two nations close together, but not without criticism from certain quarters, which urged Canadian military independence from American military affairs. Mackenzie King made more rational assessments of Soviet intentions than did Truman, and opposed American demands for improved protection in the Canadian North from Soviet attack by saying that "our best defence in the Arctic is the Arctic itself." It is nonetheless true that by April 1948, after the communists took power in Czechoslovakia, Canadian foreign policy had undergone a transformation.

St. Laurent became a proponent of a "western union" of free states, and a strong regional alliance set up under the UN charter. In 1949, Canada signed a defensive alliance with the United States, Britain, France, and eight other Western European nations. She thereby became a member of the North Atlantic Treaty Organization (NATO), a regional alliance opposed to the advance of the Communist bloc and the Warsaw Pact nations. "For us," Pearson wrote, "NATO is especially significant, as it reconciles the forces of geography and history in our national political evolution. In doing so it helps to dissipate the nightmare that used to frighten every Canadian government; a serious divergence in policy between neighbour and mother country." Canada had joined the Americans and the British in their suspicions of Russian intentions in Eastern Europe and had rejected isolationism. Canadians came to identify with the UN and NATO, and these agencies were a means whereby their government could make an essential military commitment in the name of peace. Collective security was politically acceptable to the nation as a whole, especially because the Mother Countries of the founding Canadian races were members of NATO and also because, at Pearson's suggestion, Article II of the NATO Treaty made the alliance not only a military one but also an economic, cultural, and social one. However, it was essentially a military arrangement, and Canada sent an army brigade group and twelve squadrons of the Royal Canadian Air Force to Europe and assigned her navy of about forty ships to NATO Supreme Command, where it assumed an anti-submarine role.

In continental defense and in world affairs, the press of events in the postwar era brought Canada and the United States into a closer relationship than Mackenzie King, St. Laurent, or Pearson could have imagined. Collective security had been born of necessity; it brought Canada inexorably, because of geography, into a closer relationship with the United States.

Canada's first major military role after 1945 came in response to the invasion of North Korean forces into the Republic of Korea in June 1950. Canada met her UN commitment by mobilizing a special force, which reached the Far East in December, there to fight with men from the Commonwealth, the United States, and other non-Communist countries. This demonstrated the nation's belief in the maintenance of international peace and law and order through collective security. The argument was that aggression in any part of the world constituted a threat to every other part, including Canada. In these circumstances, European defenses could not remain unprotected from the Soviet threat, and Canada sent a brigade of the Special Force to Western Europe instead of to Korea.

In Korea, the UN met the threat of Communist aggression successfully and Canada, with the third largest contingent of ground forces from UN members in the war, played an important role. For the first time in history, an international force of sixteen nations had taken the field under the flag of the UN and, for the first time (except for the defense of Hong Kong in 1941), Canadian forces had fought side by side with other countries in Asia. As Lester Pearson put it, "It meant for the first time the defeat of aggression by the armed conscience of the world." Later, Canadians would consider United States involvement in Korea a preliminary to later imperialist adventures in Vietnam, Cambodia, and Laos. But at the same time, Canadians prided themselves in contributing to collective security through the UN. As one contemporary observer of international affairs wrote, "For Canada the UN, insofar as it approximates to a system of collective security, is a rationalization of almost precisely what Canada would choose to do as a matter of policy." [14]

14. Henry F. Angus, *Canada and the Far East, 1940–1953* (Toronto: University of Toronto Press, 1953), pp. 32–33.

The Korean War found Canadians serving side by side with other soldiers from the Commonwealth. Yet three years after the peace was signed, in 1956, Commonwealth and Canadian opinion was divided on the question of cooperation during the Suez crisis. Since 1947 it had been understood among Commonwealth nations that membership in the association carried with it an obligation to inform or consult with all other members on any projected action that might affect their interest. This would allow them the opportunity of expressing their views, especially on foreign affairs. When Britain and France, and on the side of Israel, engaged in unilateral action against Egypt, preventing Colonel Nasser from seizing the Canal, and did so without consulting the Commonwealth, certain member nations were shocked and dismayed.

Canada did not condemn the action at first and only regretted it. Later, a blistering telegram sent to Number 10 Downing Street told of Ottawa's condemnation of British policy. This was official policy, but the nation was divided.

There is no way of determining how Canadian public opinion was split on the British intervention in Suez and on Canada's response. But one paper, the *Calgary Herald*, criticized the government for having run out on Britain "at a time when the United Kingdom was asserting the kind of leadership the world has missed, and needed. . . . All it did was to provide a face-saver for the Soviet puppet-dictator in Egypt and preserve his power for another day—a rank disservice to the cause of peace." Meanwhile, Australia and New Zealand lent clear support to the United Kingdom in spite of divisions within those countries, while Asian members of the Commonwealth, especially India, opposed the British intervention as high-handed "gunboat" diplomacy. Pearson rightly said at the time that the Commonwealth was "dangerously split," "on the verge of dissolution," and that his country was not a "colonial chore-boy running around shouting 'ready, aye, ready.' " But this was Pearson's view and that of his government; it was not necessarily that of the nation, where there was a considerable measure of support for the United Kingdom.

At the UN, the Anglo-French intervention was looked on as a violation of the Charter. Canada voted with the United States (then in a surly mood against Britain) and Russia in condemning the British and French. Under Pearson's leadership, which would bring him the Nobel Peace Prize, the United Nations reached a settlement and introduced a police-keeping force. Under the command of Major-General E. L. M. Burns of Canada, the UN Emergency Force supervised the evacuation of the Canal Zone. This it did successfully, and the Middle East situation had been defused, if momentarily.

Canada had acted out of self-interest in foreign affairs, particularly in Suez. It has been written that "this has generally managed to put Canada on the side of the angels." [15] It has been her policy to avoid war and to contain it, to eliminate tensions, to support international organizations and the rule of law in international affairs, to uphold the Western alliance against Communism, and to support international trade. As such it perhaps leads to "a slightly 'holier-than-thou' approach."

Yet Korea and Suez show that the government of a small nation (a "middle power," as the Canadians wished to be called in the 1950s) could play a role in world affairs. Although the great affairs of the world lay actually beyond her control, her role as "peacemaker" (although she might sometimes play the part as "powder-monkey") was a constructive one, and it was a contribution to the defense of the continent.[16] While Canadians took on an international perspective in the postwar period through this newly found role in the world, they were little aware of how North American influences were dictating their responses. Korea did not seem far away, but Suez did. They were prepared to send men and materiel to one but not to the other. They supported the United States (and the United Nations) in the one but would not support Britain and France in the other. John Foster Dulles, General Eisenhower, and Harry Truman seemed more credible to them than Sir Anthony Eden and Harold Macmillan, and at the UN they supported the United States and censured Britain and France. The era of uncertainty had come to an

15. Robert W. Reford, *Canada and Three Crises* (Ottawa: Canadian Institute of International Affairs, Contemporary Affairs Series No. 42, 1968), p. 238.

16. See J. H. Aitchison, "Canadian Foreign Policy in the House and on the Hustings," *International Journal*, XII (Autumn 1957), 278. See also James Eayrs, *Canada in World Affairs, 1955–57* (Toronto: Oxford University Press, 1959) and, edited by the same, *The Commonwealth and Suez: A Documentary Survey* (London and New York: Oxford University Press, 1964); also James M. Minifie, *Peacemaker or Powder-Monkey: Canada's Role in a Revolutionary World* (Toronto: McClelland and Stewart, 1960).

end: Canada had cast her lot with the United States and the United Nations.

This rejection of her European heritage with its French roots and British connections meant that Canada was shaping her destiny in conjunction with her great neighbor. Compromised by U.S.–Canadian military defense and war industries pacts, Canadian secretaries of state for external affairs had little scope for an independent stance among the middle powers. At the same time, her citizens would continue to be concerned with major domestic problems such as racial division, social welfare, costs and standards of living, control and use of natural resources, education, and so on. But at bottom, the American penetration of the Canadian economy, resources, and culture continue to be the major problem facing Canadian governments in the last quarter of the twentieth century. Strong nationalistic feelings are being expressed to provide controls on foreign influence in business and culture. As the Canadian economy moves toward integration with the continental economy, federal and provincial governments move slowly to introduce measures to protect Canadian identity with a minimum sacrifice to national productivity and the standard of living.

In many ways this reflects previous decisions made by governments since Confederation to ensure that Canadian national purposes are achieved, that economic and material progress is continued, that the benefits of this progress are distributed through federalism, and that the mechanisms of control and the direction of external responsibilities remain within Canadian hands. Nationhood exists with all its trials and responsibilities. However, the historic past, with its symbols, traditions, and mythology provides Canadians with support for her distinctiveness in northern North America and the world.

Suggested Readings

The best one-volume guide to available studies on Canada in French and English is Claude Thibault, *Bibliographia Canadiana* (1973). Pages 9–16 of this work list bibliographical aids, encyclopaedias, atlases, and gazettes. Also of great use are Robin W. Winks, *Recent Trends and New Literature in Canadian History* (Washington, D.C.: American Historical Association, 1959); Robin W. Winks, "Canada," in Robin W. Winks, ed., *The Historiography of the British Empire-Commonwealth* (1966); and J. L. Granatstein and Paul Stevens, eds., *Canada Since 1867: A Bibliographical Guide* (1974). Quarterly bibliographies are published in *The Canadian Historical Review* (1920 to date) and *Canadiana* (1951 to date).

GENERAL HISTORIES. There are several one-volume general histories of Canada, including W. L. Morton's *Kingdom of Canada: A General History from Earliest Times* (1969), Donald G. Creighton's *Dominion of the North: A History of Canada* (new ed., 1962); A. R. M. Lower's *Colony to Nation* (4th ed. rev. 1964), and John Bartlett Brebner, with D. C. Masters, *Canada: A Modern History* (new ed., 1970). The last of these is excellent for its study of colonial identities in the late eighteenth and nineteenth centuries. Shorter histories include Kenneth McNaught, *Pelican History of Canada* (1969), J. M. S. Careless, *Canada: A Story of Challenge* (rev. ed., 1963), and Ramsay Cook, with John T. Saywell and John C. Ricker, *Canada: a Modern Study* (1963).

BIOGRAPHIES. The work of biographical record is well underway in Canadian history. *The Dictionary of Canadian Biography/Dictionnaire biographique du Canada* (1966 to date) is a multivolume work which provides accurate and concise studies of persons who have been in Canada since 1000 A.D. It also contains useful introductory essays on special topics. Still important as a one-volume source is W. Stewart Wallace, *The Macmillan Dictionary of Canadian Biography* (1963). Other biographical works are listed in Thibault's *Bibliographia Canadiana*, pp. 22–24.

Individual biographies of interest and which make good reading are: *Samuel de Champlain* (1972) by Samuel Eliot Morison, *The Firebrand: William Lyon Mackenzie and the Rebellion in Upper Canada* (1956) by William Kilbourn, *Louis Riel* (1963) by George F. G. Stanley, and *Laurier: The First Canadian* (1965) by Joseph Schull. Canadian prime ministers since Confederation have been popular subjects for biography. Among the best of this sort are Donald G. Creighton, *John A. Macdonald* (2 vols., 1952 and 1955), Roger Graham, *Arthur Meighen: A Biography* (3 vols., 1960–1965), and Peter C. Newman, *Renegade in Power: The Diefenbaker Years*. Mackenzie King is the subject of an ongoing official biography: volume one of *William Lyon Mackenzie King* was written by R. MacGregor Dawson (1958); volume two, by H. Blair Neatby (1963). *The Mackenzie King Record* (1960 to date) and *Mike: The Memoirs of the Right Honourable Lester Pearson* (1973 to date) are multivolume records of two prominent politicians of the twentieth century.

TOPICAL STUDIES. W. A. Mackintosh, "Economic Factors in Canadian History," *Canadian Historical Review*, IV (March 1923), provides a beginning point for the study of environment and economic development in Canada. W. T. Easterbrook and H. G. J. Aitken's *Canadian Economic History* (1956) is a text of lasting significance for the colonial period but should be read in connection with R. Cole Harris and John Warkentin's *Canada Before Confederation* (1974), a study in historical geography. Harold Innis' *Fur Trade of Canada: An Introduction to Canadian Economic History* (1930; rev. ed. 1956) and his *The Cod Fisheries: The History of an International Economy* (1940) show how Canada developed in relation to European demands for staples. Donald G. Creighton's *Commercial Empire of the St. Lawrence, 1760–1850* (1937) demonstrates the importance of the great river in the political and economic development of Canada. Numerous histories of corporations exist, as do studies of agriculture, lumbering, fishing, and the like. These are listed in *Bibliographia Canadiana*.

Canadian frontier experiences are a subject of continued interest in identifying the myths and symbols of the Canadian experience. J. M. S.

Careless' "Frontierism, Metropolitanism and Canadian History," *Canadian Historical Review*, XXXV (1954) outlines the various schools of Canadian historiography and argues that urban dominance over a rural hinterland is central to the national past. Comparisons with other frontiers are drawn in Paul Sharp's "Three Frontiers: Some Comparative Studies of Canadian, American, and Australian Settlement," *Pacific Historical Review*, XXIV (1955).

No one-volume study exists on the use and control of the seas in relation to Canadian development. However, Gerald S. Graham, *Empire of the North Atlantic: The Maritime Struggle for North America* (rev. ed. 1958) and Barry M. Gough, *The Royal Navy and the Northwest Coast of North America, 1810–1914: A Study of British Maritime Ascendancy* (1971) point to the importance of sea power in relation to imperial interests on the Atlantic and Pacific coasts, respectively. Of numerous studies dealing with the evolution of Canada's defense policy, the following are recommended: Richard A. Preston, *Canada and "Imperial Defense": A Study of the Origins of the British Commonwealth's Defense Organization, 1867–1919* (1967) and Charles P. Stacey, *Arms, Men and Governments: The War Policies of Canada, 1939–1945* (1970).

With respect to French Canada, two introductory works are highly recommended: Marcel Trudel, *Introduction to New France* (1968) and W. J. Eccles, *France in America* (1972). The most recent studies of Lower Canada after the conquest are Fernand Ouellet's *Histoire économique et sociale de Québec, 1760–1850: structures et conjecture* (1968) and, by the same author, *Éléments d'histoire sociale du Bas-Canada* (1972). Other important works are Jean Pierre Wallot and John Hare's *Confrontations: choix de textes sur les problems politiques, économiques et sociaux du Bas-Canada, 1806–1810* (1968) and Jean Hamelin and Yves Roby's *Histoire économique du Québec 1851–1896* (1968). No comparable studies have been undertaken for Quebec in the twentieth century, but of general interest are Ramsey Cook's *Canada and the French Canadian Question* (1966) and his *The Maple Leaf Forever: Essays on Nationalism and Politics in Canada* (1971).

The eighteen-volume *Canadian Centenary Series: A History of Canada* (1963 to date) will be, when completed, the most extensive multi-volume history of Canada bearing on the themes of political and national development, though not neglecting social and economic themes. Extensive bibliographies are contained in most volumes. Edited by W. L. Morton and Donald G. Creighton, the series begins with T. J. Oleson's *Early Voyages and Northern Approaches, 1000–1632*. Other volumes published or planned are Marcel Trudel's *The Beginnings of New France, 1524–*

1663, W. J. Eccles' *Canada under Louis XIV, 1669–1701*, Jean Blain's *New France, 1702–1734*, G. F. G. Stanley's *New France 1744–1760*, Hilda Neatby's *Quebec, 1760–1791*, Gerald M. Craig's *Upper Canada, 1784–1841*, Fernand Ouellet's *Lower Canada, 1792–1841*, W. S. MacNutt's *The Atlantic Provinces, 1712–1857*, J. M. S. Careless' *The Union of the Canadas, 1841–1857*, E. E. Rich's *The Fur Trade and the Northwest to 1857*, W. L. Morton's *The Critical Years, 1857–1873*, P. B. Waite's *Canada, 1874–1896*, R. Craig Brown and G. R. Cook's *Canada, 1896–1921*, Roger Graham's *Canada, 1922–1939*, Morris Zaslow's *The Opening of the Canadian North, 1870–1914*, Morris Zaslow's *The North, 1914–1967*, and D. G. Creighton's *Canada, 1939–1967*. Because these volumes do not always deal satisfactorily with certain provinces, the reader's attention is drawn to Margaret Ormsby's *British Columbia: A History* (1958) and W. L. Morton's *Manitoba: A History* (2nd ed., 1968). These books are worth reading in their own right.

Canada's external relations are surveyed in G. P. de T. Glazebrook, *History of Canadian External Relations* (rev. ed., 2 vols., 1966). Of particular interest is C. P. Stacey, "The Myth of the Unguarded Frontier, 1815–1871," *American Historical Review*, LVI (1950), S. F. Wise and R. Craig Brown, *Canada Views the United States: Nineteenth Century Political Attitudes* (1967), Gerald M. Craig, *The United States and Canada* (1968), and James Eayrs, *In Defence of Canada* (1964 to date), a multivolume survey of Canadian foreign policy since 1919. Two series, *The Relations of Canada and the United States*, J. T. Shotwell, ed. (25 vols., 1936–1945) and *Canada in World Affairs* (1941 to date) provide much information and important surveys of Canada's relations with the world, especially the British Commonwealth and the United States.

Cultural identity of Canadians was first investigated in W. Stewart Wallace's *Growth of Canadian National Feeling* (1927), a period piece now outdated. W. L. Morton's *The Canadian Identity* (2nd ed., 1972) describes the main thrusts of Canada's character in relation to Europe and the United States. William Kilbourn's *Canada: A Guide to the Peaceable Kingdom* (1970) is the best of numerous anthologies dealing with Canadian life styles and attitudes. Among the best one-volume studies of Canada's lands, peoples, and character, with due reference to the West and North, is George Woodcock's *Canada and the Canadians* (rev. ed., 1973). Of related interest are A. R. M. Lower's *Canadians in the Making* (1958), Mason Wade's *The French Canadians, 1760–1967* (2 vols., 1967), E. Palmer Patterson's *The Canadian Indian: A History since 1500* (1972), and Robin W. Winks' *The Blacks in Canada* (1972).

Index